欢迎:中学汉语课本

HUANYING
An Invitation to Chinese Workbook

JIAYING HOWARD AND LANTING XU

VOLUME 1
1
2
PART 2

Cheng & Tsui Company
Boston

Huanying Volume 1 Part 2 Workbook

19 18 17 16 15 14 13   4 5 6 7 8 9 10 11 12

First edition 2009

Published by
Cheng & Tsui Company, Inc.
25 West Street
Boston, MA 02111-1213 USA
Fax (617) 426-3669
www.cheng-tsui.com
"Bringing Asia to the World"™

ISBN 978-0-88727-705-4

Illustrations by Landong Xu, Qiguang Xu and Augustine Liu

Workbook design by Linda Robertson

Chinese text editor: Jing Wu

Printed in the United States of America

CONTENTS

AUDIO RECORDINGS

Throughout this workbook, you will see an audio CD icon to the left of many of the exercises. Audio CD icons indicate the presence of audio recordings, which are available as downloadable audio files. For information on how to download the audio files for this workbook, please see p. iv of your Volume 1 Textbook.

第四单元　日常用品

UNIT 4　Things We Use Every Day

4.1　这是谁的书包？
Whose Backpack Is This?

一．听力练习　LISTENING PRACTICE

I. Dictation. Listen carefully to Audio Clip 4-1-1. Each sentence will be read twice, first at normal speed for you to get a general idea, and then at slow speed for you to write down the sentence in pinyin.

1. _____

2. _____

3. _____

4. _____

5. _____

II. Listen carefully to Audio Clip 4-1-2 and then place tone marks above each character in the poem.

一 去 二 三 里，烟 村 四 五 家。

亭 台 六 七 座，八 九 十 枝 花。

III. Listen to Dialogue 1 from Lesson 4.1 and then answer the True/False questions in Audio Clip 4-1-3.

	1	2	3
对			
错			

 IV. Listen to Dialogue 2 from Lesson 4.1 and then answer the True/False questions in Audio Clip 4-1-4.

	1	2	3
对			
错			

V. Listen carefully to the questions in Audio Clip 4-1-5 and write your answers in complete sentences in the space below.

1. _____

2. _____

3. _____

4. _____

5. _____

VI. Listen to Audio Clip 4-1-6 and match the color you hear with the object that usually comes in that color.

1. _____   2. _____   3. _____   4. _____

5. _____   6. _____   7. _____

二. 综合语言练习   INTEGRATED LANGUAGE PRACTICE

I. **How do you say it in Chinese?**

1. his backpack

_____

2. her name

_____

3. David's dog

_____

4. a new company

_____

5. old toys

_____

6. Is this your backpack?

_____

7. Is your dog black or brown?

_____

8. This is your computer, right?

_____

9. Whose backpack could this be?

_____

10. Could this cat be Maria's?

_____

II. Pair Activity: At the "Lost and Found" Counter

Student A

You misplaced your backpack at break today. Now you are at the school's "Lost & Found" counter to see if anyone has turned in your backpack. You start the conversation by asking: 这儿有我的书包吗？ The staff at the counter (played by your partner) will then ask you some questions about your backpack. Answer the questions based on the information on your "Lost & Found" card.

```
                 LOST & FOUND INFORMATION CARD
       (PLEASE FILL OUT AS MUCH INFORMATION AS YOU CAN REMEMBER)
```

丢的东西的名称: 书包	有没有你的名字? 没有
丢的时间: 今天上午	大小? 大
新旧? 旧	颜色? 绿色
内容? 有我的生物书.	

Word Bank

1. 丢 diū, to lose	2. 内容 nèiróng, content	3. 名称 míngchēng, name of an item or product
4. 东西 dōngxī, things	5. 生物 shēngwù, biology	

Student B

You work for the school's "Lost & Found" counter. Now a student (played by your partner) is asking you if anyone found his/her backpack. Ask your partner the following questions to find out the specifics of the backpack. Listen to his/her answers carefully and record the results in the space next to each question.

1. 你的书包是大的还是小的? _____

2. 你的书包是绿色的还是蓝色的? _____

3. 你的书包是新的还是旧的? _____

4. 你的书包上有你的名字吗? _____

5. 你的书包里有生物书还是历史书? _____

6. 给你，你的书包在这儿呢。_____

III. Pair Activity: Help a Lost Child

Student A

You are trying to help a child who seems to have gotten lost and is crying on the street. Ask the child (played by your partner) questions to find out information about his/her house. Listen to his/her answers carefully and record them in the space given.

你家的房子是新的还是旧的？_____

你家的房子是大还是小？_____

你家的房子是白色的还是红色的？_____

你家的狗住在大房子还是小房子里？_____

狗的房子是蓝色的还是绿色的？_____

小朋友，你看，这个是不是你的家？_____

Student B

You are a three-year-old who, while chasing your dog, ran out of the house and got lost. A pedestrian (played by your partner) is trying to take you back to your home. He/she will ask you some questions about your house. Listen to his/her questions carefully and answer them according to the following description:

你住在一个很大也很新的红房子里。你家的狗住在一个绿色的小房子里。

IV. Pair Activity: Good Companion

Situation 1: Shopping Online for a Gift

Student A

You are trying to buy a birthday gift online for your little sister, and you have asked a friend (played by your partner) to shop with you. Ask your friend for his/her opinion on the items that you have selected. Your friend will comment on them, using the expression "太…了".

Model: **A:** 你觉得这个书包怎么样？   **B:** 太难看了！

The items displayed on your computer screen are:

	zìxíngchē	wáwa	diànzi yóuxìjī
书包	自行车	娃娃	电子游戏机

Student B

Your friend (played by your partner) wants to ask for your expert opinion on the possible gifts that he/she has selected for his/her little sister's birthday. Comment on the items that your partner selected, using 太…了.

Situation 2: At a Garage Sale

You have accompanied your friend (played by your partner) to a garage sale. There is a lot of stuff — used and new — scattered on a large picnic table.

		zìxíngchē	diànziyóuxìjī
书包	电脑	自行车	电子游戏机

Student A

You are interested in buying the items shown above. Show the items that you are interested in to your friend and ask for his/her opinion.

Model: A: 这个书包怎么样?
 B: 太难看了!

Student B

Your friend wants to buy several things. Look at the items (above) that your friend has selected and give your opinion on them, using 太···了.

Model: A: 这个书包怎么样?
 B: 太难看了!

V. **Pair Activity: What Color Is It?**

Step 1: If you could own the following luxury goods, what color would you like them to be? Write down the color next to each item.

1. fángzi

房子, house _____

2. zìxíngchē

自行车, bike _____

3. chuán

船, boat _____

4. fēijī

飞机, airplane _____

5. qìchē

汽车, car _____

Step 2: Ask your partner what color he/she would like his/her luxury goods to be, and record his/her answers in complete sentences below.

Model: **A:** 你的房子是什么颜色的？
　　　　 B: 我的房子是蓝（色）的。

1. _____

2. _____

3. _____

4. _____

5. _____

VI. Match Them!

Match the characters in Column A with pinyin pronunciations in Column B and English meanings in Column C.

Column A	Column B	Column C
蓝(色)	zhèr	green
新书包	xīn shūbāo	a particle to express mood
绿(色)	fàng	blue
让	yòng	old toy
啊	à	here
这儿	jiù wánjù	put, place
原来	ràng	originally
用	lán(sè)	let, allow
放	yuánlái	new school bag
旧玩具	lǜ(sè)	use

VII. Word Hunt

Following the clues, find the Chinese character sentences hidden in the crossword puzzle below.

生	文	健	这	个	放	书	玩	具	学	中	文	书	丽	马
五	学	身	个	是	啊	，	我	的	书	包	在	这	儿	！
让	生	！	电	。	你	妹	妹	的	。	看	们	个	园	来
我	的	电	脑	是	新	的	。	原	来	是	妹	妹	的	。
看	他	的	我	这	。	琴	钢	来	十	黄	电	脑	影	司
看	蓝	色	程	个	绿	们	他	琴	几	包	多	少	弟	哥
！	海	伦	的	房	子	是	白	的	，	不	是	蓝	的	。
电	。	书	表	子	色	。	字	！	语	不	文	忙	雷	马
影	下	旧	三	太	就	公	四	狗	我	们	是	丽	凯	娅
上	中	在	早	旧	！	八	弟	。	新	好	的	我	！	儿
。	午	那	玩	了	用	它	放	我	的	玩	具	。	的	玩
是	星	期	！	。	玛	丽	亚	有	一	个	红	书	包	。

Clues:

1. Maria has a red backpack.

2. This is your piano, not mine.

3. Helen's（海伦）house is white, not blue.

4. My computer is new.

5. This house is really run down.

6. (It) used to belong to my younger sister.

7. Ah, here is my backpack!

8. Let me see!

9. (I) put my toys inside it.

三．汉字练习 CHINESE CHARACTER PRACTICE

I. **Write the characters in the correct stroke order.**

lán	艹	一 十 艹 艹 艹 艹 艹 薜 薜 莘 莘 蓝 蓝 (13)
蓝	蓝 蓝 蓝	
bāo	勹	丿 勹 匀 匀 包 (5)
包	包 包 包	
lǜ	纟	乙 纟 纟 纟 纟 纪 绉 绿 绿 绿 (11)
绿	绿 绿 绿	
xīn	斤	丶 亠 辛 立 立 辛 亲 亲 新 新 新 (13)
新	新 新 新	
jiù	日	丨 刂 旧 旧 旧 (5)
旧	旧 旧 旧	
ràng	讠	丶 讠 讣 让 让 (5)
让	让 让 让	
yuán	厂	一 厂 厂 厂 厉 厉 原 原 原 原 (10)
原	原 原 原	
lái	木	一 丆 丆 立 平 来 来 (7)
来	来 来 来	
tài	大	一 ナ 大 太 (4)
太	太 太 太	
fàng	攵	丶 亠 方 方 放 放 放 放 (8)
放	放 放 放	
jù	八	丨 刂 日 日 目 且 具 具 (8)
具	具 具 具	

4.2 我带书去学校
I Take Books to School

一. 听力练习 LISTENING PRACTICE

I. Dictation. Listen carefully to Audio Clip 4-2-1. Each sentence will be read twice, first at normal speed for you to get a general idea, and then at slow speed for you to write down the sentence in pinyin.

1._____

2._____

3._____

4._____

5._____

II. Listen to Audio Clip 4-2-2 carefully and then place tone marks above each character in the poem.

墙 角 数 枝 梅，凌 寒 独 自 开。

遥 知 不 是 雪，为 有 暗 香 来。

III. Listen to Dialogue 1 from Lesson 4.2 and then answer the True/False questions in Audio Clip 4-2-3.

	1	2	3	4
对				
错				

IV. Listen to Dialogue 2 from Lesson 4.2 and then answer the True/False questions in Audio Clip 4-2-4.

	1	2	3
对			
错			

 V. Rejoinders: What would be the most appropriate responses to the questions you hear in Audio Clip 4-2-5? Circle the correct answers from the choices below.

Question 1

A. 对。你呢？

B. 三本。

C. 好，我带一本。

Question 2

A. 是。你呢？

B. 蜡笔是红色的。

C. 对。

Question 3

A. 对不起，我没有汉语课本。

B. 啊，我的汉语课本在这儿！

C. 丁老师有汉语课本。

Question 4

A. 对。你呢？

B. 好。你带吧。

C. 你看，我有数学书和三本化学书。

Question 5

A. 你的笔是黑色的。

B. 你看看妮娜有没有。

C. 这不是红笔。

VI. Listen to the questions in Audio Clip 4-2-6 carefully and write your answers in complete sentences.

1. _____

2. _____

3. _____

4. _____

5. _____

VII. Listen carefully to Audio Clip 4-2-7 and see what Tom, Maria and Kelly need to bring to school tomorrow; then fill out the table below.

	课本	练习本/本子	蜡笔	电脑	笔
汤姆					
玛丽娅					
凯丽					

二. 综合语言练习 INTEGRATED LANGUAGE PRACTICE

I. **How do you say it in Chinese?**

Section 1: Phrases

1. five textbooks

_____

2. three notebooks

_____

3. one computer

_____

4. two boxes of crayons

_____

5. two red pens

_____

6. three dogs

_____

7. one younger sister

_____

8. one cat

_____

9. five classes

_____

10. two backpacks

_____

Section 2: Sentences

1. How many textbooks will you bring on Wednesday?

_____

2. How many black pens do you have?

_____

3. May I use your Chinese textbook?

_____

4. Would you like to use a red pen?

_____

5. Does he bring that many crayons to school every day?

_____

II. Pair Activity: Are You Ready for School?

Situation 1: Student Mentor

Student A

This semester you will work as a student mentor to a freshman, who just arrived in China from Canada. Today is the first day of Freshmen Orientation. Your responsibility is to check if the new student has his/her class materials ready. Go over the course material checklist with the new student (played by your partner) and check in the box if he/she has the item.

Model: A: 你有汉语课本吗？   **or:**   A: 你有汉语课本吗？

B: 有。   B: 还没有。

A: 你有几本？   A: 请你今天去买，
                                                 好吗？

B: 我有两本。   B: 好。

Word Bank

1. 买 mǎi to buy	2. 文具 wénjù stationary

今年要用的课本和文具	
有√	课本和文具
	汉语课本（两本）
	数学课本（一本）
	英语课本（五本）
	美术课本（一本）
	历史课本（一本）
	练习本（五本）
	蜡笔（两盒）

Student B

You are a freshman at the Shanghai International School. The school has assigned you a student mentor, whose job is to help you adjust to the life at the school as well as in China. Today is the first day of Freshmen Orientation. Your mentor (played by your partner) would like to check if you have all the class materials ready. Listen to his/her questions carefully and answer the questions based on your own checklist.

Model: **A:** 你有汉语课本吗?   **or:** **A:** 你有汉语课本吗?

 B: 有。   **B:** 还没有。

 A: 你有几本?   **A:** 请你今天去买,
           好吗?

 B: 我有两本。   **B:** 好。

Word Bank

1. 买 mǎi to buy	2. 文具 wénjù stationary

今年要用的课本和文具	
有√	课本和文具
√	汉语课本（两本）
√	数学课本（一本）
	英语课本（五本）
	美术课本（一本）
√	历史课本（一本）
√	练习本（五本）
	蜡笔（两盒）

Situation 2: Are You Ready for the Chinese Class?

Student A

You are a transfer student at the Shanghai International School. Now your classmate is going over the Chinese language course material list with you. Listen to his/her questions carefully and answer the questions based on your own checklist.

Model:	A: 你有汉语课本吗?	**or:**	A: 你有汉语课本吗?
	B: 有。		B: 还没有。
	A: 你有几本?		A: 请你今天去买,好吗?
	B: 我有两本。		B: 好。

汉语课的课本和文具	
有✓	课本和文具
✓	汉语课本（两本）
	汉字练习本（四本）
✓	练习本（一本）
	蜡笔（两盒）
✓	红色和黑色笔（两支）

Student B

You are a student at the Shanghai International School. Now you are talking to a transfer student to see if he/she has all the required course materials for the Chinese language class. Go over the course material list with your student (played by your partner). Check the box if he/she has the materials.

Model: **A:** 你有汉语课本吗？ **or:** **A:** 你有汉语课本吗？

B: 有。 **B** 还没有。

A: 你有几本？ **A:** 请你今天去买，
好吗？

B: 我有两本。 **B:** 好。

汉语课的课本和文具	
有√	课本和文具
	汉语课本（两本）
	汉字练习本（四本）
	练习本（一本）
	蜡笔（两盒）
	红色和黑色笔（两支）

III. Character Bingo

Step 1: Choose 16 words from the word bank and write them at random, with one in each square on the game board.

Step 2: Pair up with a partner, take turns reading one term at a time from the word bank. Cross out each term as you read it. When your partner calls out a term, listen carefully, and if you have that term written in a square, cross it out with an X while telling your partner: "我有…"

Remember: You are calling your partner's bingo game and he is calling yours. The first player to cross out four terms in a row (horizontally, vertically or across) is the winner. The winner should call out: "中了！" (zhòng le, "I won").

Word Bank

红色	蓝色	绿色	黑色	颜色
蜡笔	书包	练习本	课本	用
名字	原来	玩具	放	新
旧	这儿	那么	几个	本子

Bingo Grid

IV. Mixer Activity: Find Your Classmate

Imagine that you are at the Freshman Social. You would like to get to know someone who's taking the same classes and using the same class materials as you. Walk around the classroom and ask your classmates questions based on the information below. Once you find someone who is taking the same classes and using the same books as you, write the student's name in the space given below.

Card A	Card B
你这个学期上英语，汉语，化学和经济。 你用的课本有： 化学 两本 汉语 两本 经济 一本 英语 五本	你这个学期上英语，汉语，化学和经济。 你用的课本有： 化学 一本 汉语 三本 经济 一本 英语 五本
Card C	Card D
你这个学期上经济，历史，英语AP和法语。 你用的课本有： 经济 两本 历史 两本 英语AP 十本 法语 三本	你这个学期上美国历史，汉语，物理和数学。 你用的课本有： 美国历史 两本 汉语 两本 物理 两本 数学 两本

Card E

你这个学期上中国历史，
物理，美术和经济。
你用的课本有：
中国历史 一本
汉语 两本
物理 一本
数学 三本

Card F

你这个学期上数学，历史，
英语和化学。
你用的课本有：
化学 两本
数学 一本
历史 三本
英语 五本

Card G

你这个学期上数学，历史，
英语和化学。
你用的课本有：
化学 两本
数学 两本
历史 一本
英语 四本

Card H

你这个学期上经济，历史，
英语AP和法语。
你用的课本有：
经济 两本
历史 三本
英语AP 十本
法语 两本

Card I	**Card J**
你这个学期上美国历史，汉语，物理和数学。 你用的课本有： 美国历史 两本 汉语 两本 物理 一本 数学 一本	你这个学期上中国历史，物理，美术和经济。 你用的课本有： 中国历史 两本 汉语 两本 物理 两本 数学 一本

V. **Pair Activity: What's in Your School Bag?**

Step 1: Open your school bag and see what's inside. Then write a list of the things in your school bag.

_____

_____

_____

_____

_____

_____

_____

Step 2: Pair up with a classmate. Tell each other what's in your school bag.

Model: 我有数学书、汉语书、三本练习本、四支笔……

When your partner reports, listen carefully and write down what you hear in the space below.

_____

_____

_____

_____

_____

_____

_____

_____

VI. Group or Pair Activity: What Will You Bring to My House?

Suppose your friend has invited you over to his house for the day. After throwing the dice, the player needs to say "我带 _____ 去你家". Please be as specific as possible. If a player cannot say the sentence correctly, s/he may not advance.

22.	21.	20.	19. ◀
FINISH			
	GO TO THE FINISH		

14. ▶	15.	16.	17.	18. ▲
			SKIP ONE SPACE	

13. ▲	12.	11.	10.	9. ◀
	BACK TO 6			

4. ▶	5.	6.	7.	8. ▲
SKIP ONE SPACE			**LOSE A TURN**	

3. ▲	2.	1.	**START** ◀	

VII. Match Them!

Match the characters in Column A with pinyin pronunciations in Column B and English meanings in Column C.

Column A	Column B	Column C
带课本	hé	so many
几本书	hēi làbǐ	how many books
借本子	hóngsè	color
练习本	zhǐ	only
那么多	dài kèběn	box (can be used as a measure word)
盒	jiè běnzi	black crayon
黑蜡笔	jǐ běn shū	borrow notebook
支	zhī	a measure word for pens
颜色	nàme duō	red color, red
红色	yánsè	notebook
只	liànxíběn	take, take along a textbook

三. 汉字练习　CHINESE CHARACTER PRACTICE

姓名：＿＿＿＿＿＿＿＿＿＿＿

I. Write the characters in the correct stroke order.

dài 巾	一 十 卄 卅 卅 世 带 带 带 (9)
带 带 带 带	

běn 木	一 十 才 木 本 (5)
本 本 本 本	

liàn 纟	㇂ 纟 纟 纟 纡 纩 练 练 (8)
练 练 练 练	

nà 阝	丁 丮 𠃌 𦐂 那 那 (6)
那 那 那 那	

hé 皿	丿 人 𠆢 𠆢 合 合 合 合 盒 盒 盒 (11)
盒 盒 盒 盒	

là 虫	丶 冂 口 中 虫 虫 虫 虾 蚰 蚰 蜡 蜡 蜡 蜡 (14)
蜡 蜡 蜡 蜡	

bǐ 竹	丿 𠂉 𠂉 𠂉 竹 竺 竺 笔 笔 笔 (10)
笔 笔 笔 笔	

jiè 亻	丿 亻 亻 𠆢 𠆢 供 供 借 借 借 (10)
借 借 借 借	

zhī 支	一 十 𠧘 支 (4)
支 支 支 支	

yán 页	丶 丷 亠 亠 立 产 产 彦 彦 彦 彦 颜 颜 颜 颜 (15)
颜 颜 颜 颜	

sè	色										ノ ク 각 名 乒 色 (6)
色	色	色	色								

hóng	纟										ㄥ 纟 纟 纟 红 红 (6)
红	红	红	红								

hēi	黑										丨 冂 冂 冂 四 四 甲 里 黑 黑 黑 (12)
黑	黑	黑	黑								

4.3 买文具
Buying School Supplies

一. 听力练习 **LISTENING PRACTICE**

I. Phrase Dictation. Listen carefully to Audio Clip 4-3-1. Each phrase will be read twice, first at normal speed for you to get a general idea, and then at slow speed for you to write down the phrase in pinyin.

1. _____

2. _____

3. _____

4. _____

5. _____

II. Sentence Dictation. Listen carefully to Audio Clip 4-3-2. Each sentence will be read twice, first at normal speed for you to get a general idea, and then at slow speed for you to write down the sentence in pinyin.

1. _____

2. _____

3. _____

4. _____

5. _____

III. Listen carefully to Audio Clip 4-3-3 and then place tone marks above each character in the poem.

锄 禾 日 当 午，汗 滴 禾 下 土。

谁 知 盘 中 餐，粒 粒 皆 辛 苦。

IV. Listen to Audio Clip 4-3-4 and write a shopping list for Kelly.

凯丽要买什么

	名称 Item	数量 Quantity
1.		
2.		
3.		
4.		

V. Mary, Tom, Tony and Linda are going shopping for school supplies. Listen to the dialogue in Audio Clip 4-3-5 and find out what each person would like to buy. Please mark the items in the table below.

玛丽									
汤姆									
安东尼									
林达									

VI. Listen to the questions in Audio Clip 4-3-6 and answer them in complete sentences. You can write your answers in pinyin or Chinese characters.

1. _____

2. _____

3. _____

4. _____

5. _____

二. 综合语言练习 INTEGRATED LANGUAGE PRACTICE

I. How do you say it in Chinese?

Section 1: Phrases

1. two blue rulers

_____

2. one red ballpoint pen

_____

3. twenty yellow file folders

_____

4. three kinds of notebooks

_____

5. six purple erasers

_____

6. ten blue MP3 Players

_____

7. one box of yellow crayons

_____

8. a dozen red pencils

_____

9. five white notebooks

_____

10. two black backpacks

_____

Section 2: Sentences

1. OK, I'll buy a green one.

_____

2. The Chinese like the color red, right?

_____

3. May I look at that purple file folder?

_____

4. It's nice, but rather big (for me). I'd like to have a smaller one.

_____

5. Look, there are MP3 players here.

_____

6. We have white erasers and rulers. Would you like to buy them?

_____

7. Let's take a look over there!

_____

8. I'd like to buy a few ballpoint pens.

_____

II. Pair Activity: Taking Inventory

You are volunteering at Shanghai Resource Center for Teachers, a non-profit agency that distributes donated educational supplies to educators in remote parts of China. Your job today is to unpack, sort and count donated goods. Team up with your partner and take turns filling out the inventory sheets.

Student A

Step 1: You start by telling your partner the contents of the box that you opened. Make sure that you tell your partner the name, quantity and color of each item in the box.

Model: 第一个箱子有十个本子，两个黄色的，八个白色的。

第一个箱子：

名字	数量	颜色
文件夹	35个	黄色20个，红色15个
铅笔	100支	黑色20支，红色25支，紫色25支，黄色25支，绿色5支
练习本	40本	蓝色5本，绿色32本，红色3本
尺子	17把	白色5把，浅蓝色8把，粉色4把
橡皮	29块	灰色16块，红色7块，紫色6块

Now it's your turn to fill out the inventory list. Listen to your partner carefully and write down the contents of the second box.

第二个箱子：

名字	数量	颜色

Student B

Step 2: You start by filling out the inventory list according to what your partner tells you. Make sure that you record the name, quantity and color of each item that you hear.

第一个箱子：

名字	数量	颜色

Now it's your turn to tell your partner the content of the box that you opened. Make sure that you tell your partner the name, quantity and color of each item in the box.

Model: 第一个箱子有十个本子，两个黄色的，八个白色的。

第二个箱子：

名字	数量	颜色
铅笔	50支	黑色20支，红色30支
尺子	22把	白色3把，浅蓝色19把
橡皮	62块	蓝色18块，绿色22块，紫色10块，黄色10块
文件夹	88个	白色40个，红色12个，绿色18个，蓝色18个
练习本	55本	灰色16本，红色9本，白色15本，蓝色15本

⦀ Small Group Activity: Buying School Supplies

You and your classmates are going shopping for school supplies together. In order to get a bulk discount, you decide to pay together and then divide the items up once you are back home. This means that you don't necessarily get the item in your desired color in the end!

Divide into groups of four. Choose one person from the group as the leader. S/he "picks out" items that you bought from the shopping bag and asks who would like to have them. Listen carefully to the items being called out and let the leader know if you want them, how many and in which color. Once you claim an item, record it (with name of the item, quantity and color) in your log so that you can pay later.

Model: Leader: 谁要红色的圆珠笔？
Person 1: 我要两支。
Person 2: 我要三支。

Word Bank

买到   mǎidào   purchased

第一个人：

你要买：三本绿色的练习本，两支黑色圆珠笔，两支红色圆珠笔，和五个蓝色文件夹。

你买到：＿＿＿＿＿＿＿＿＿＿＿＿＿＿＿＿＿＿＿

第二个人：

你要买：两本蓝色练习本，一把尺子，两块黑白色的橡皮，一个红色文件夹。

你买到：＿＿＿＿＿＿＿＿＿＿＿＿＿＿＿＿＿＿＿

第三个人：

你要买：五个黄色文件夹，两本紫色的练习本，两盒蜡笔，十支铅笔，四支红圆珠笔。

你买到：＿＿＿＿＿＿＿＿＿＿＿＿＿＿＿＿＿＿＿

第四个人：

你要买：两把白色的尺子，一块紫橡皮，三支红铅笔，两支黄铅笔，和两支蓝铅笔。

你买到：＿＿＿＿＿＿＿＿＿＿＿＿＿＿＿＿＿＿＿

Group Leader:

The right column lists the different kinds of supplies that you have bought. When you ask questions, you can pick up a color from the left column to add it to the name of the item.

Model: 谁要黑色的文件夹?
谁要黄色的文件夹?

颜色		文具	
红色	黄色	文件夹	练习本
黑色	紫色	尺子	橡皮
蓝色	白色	铅笔	圆珠笔
		蜡笔	

IV. **Mixer Activity: Test Your Sixth Sense**

Step 1: Circle one statement from each of the following lists that best describes you. Later, you will be interviewed by your classmates.

1. 我喜欢红色。
我喜欢蓝色。
我喜欢紫色。
我喜欢黑色。
我喜欢白色。

2. 我每天带很多课本去学校。
我每天带很多笔去学校。
我每天带两个练习本去学校。
我每天带三块橡皮去学校。
我每天带一把尺子去学校。

3. 我没有MP3播放器。
   我有MP3播放器。
   我要买MP3播放器。

4. 我不喜欢MP3播放器。
   我喜欢MP3播放器，可是妈妈不让我买。

5. 我的书包是黑色的。
   我的书包是蓝色的。
   我的书包是紫色的。
   我的书包是绿色的。
   我的书包是红色的。

Step 2: Walk around the classroom and interview at least three classmates, using the 是不是 question form. Try to ask different questions to different students based on your observation of their likes, dislikes and habits. Listen carefully to their answers and record them in the chart below.

Model:

Possible questions:	Possible answers:
你是不是喜欢蓝色？	是啊！你真神了！★
你是不是不喜欢MP3播放器？	不是，我很喜欢，可是妈妈不让我买。

★你真神了！ Nǐ zhēn shén le! You are such a wonder!

学生姓名：	
喜欢的颜色	
每天带去学校的东西	
有没有MP3	
书包的颜色	

学生姓名：	
喜欢的颜色	
每天带去学校的东西	
有没有MP3	
书包的颜色	

学生姓名：	
喜欢的颜色	
每天带去学校的东西	
有没有MP3	
书包的颜色	

V. Pinyin Crossword Puzzle

Translate the clues and complete the crossword puzzle in pinyin.

Across:

1. red
2. green
4. beige
5. backpack
6. purple
8. ruler
9. pink
12. orange
13. textbook
15. white
16. ball pen
17. file folder

Down:

1. yellow
2. blue
3. eraser
6. brown
7. notebook
10. pencil
11. black
14. crayon

VI. Complete the Dialogue

Suppose you are in a store and the salesperson asks you the following questions. How are you going to answer?

A: 你要买什么？

B: _____

A: 我们有红的，绿的，蓝的，紫的。你要哪个颜色的？

B: _____

A: 你要不要练习本？这种练习本很好看，你买几本吧！

B: _____

A: 现在很多人喜欢用紫色的圆珠笔。你要不要看看？

B: _____

VII. Match Them!

Match the characters in Column A with pinyin pronunciations in Column B and English meanings in Column C.

Column A	Column B	Column C
买	bái	pencil
文具	wénjiànjiā	ball-point pen
种	kuài	purple
黄	dà	eraser
白	zǐ	buy
紫	mǎi	type, kind
铅笔	MP sān bōfàngqì	white
圆珠笔	wénjù	file folder
橡皮	yuánzhūbǐ	yellow
尺（子）	qiānbǐ	MP3 player
块	bǎ	stationary
把	zhǒng	ruler
文件夹	chǐ(zi)	a measure word
大	huáng	big
MP3播放器	xiàngpí	a measure word (piece)

三. 汉字练习 CHINESE CHARACTER PRACTICE

姓名：_____

I. Write the characters in the correct stroke order.

mǎi	一			ー ア 勹 罕 买 买 (6)
买	买	买	买	
wén	文			、 一 ナ 文 (4)
文	文	文	文	
zhǒng	禾			ノ 二 千 禾 禾 禾 利 和 种 (9)
种	种	种	种	
huáng	黄			一 十 廿 艹 芏 莊 苎 苗 苗 黄 黄 (11)
黄	黄	黄	黄	
bái	白			ノ 亻 白 白 白 (5)
白	白	白	白	
zǐ	糸			ノ 匕 止 止 此 此 些 紫 紫 紫 紫 (12)
紫	紫	紫	紫	
qiān	钅			ノ 𠂉 𠂆 𠂉 钅 钅 钌 铅 铅 铅 (10)
铅	铅	铅	铅	
yuán	口			丨 冂 冂 冃 冃 冏 圁 圆 圆 圆 (10)
圆	圆	圆	圆	
zhū	王			一 二 千 王 王 玎 珍 玞 珠 珠 (10)
珠	珠	珠	珠	
xiàng	木			一 十 才 木 朾 栌 柠 栌 栌 橡 橡 橡 橡 (15)
橡	橡	橡	橡	

pí	皮							ㄱ 厂 广 广 皮 (5)
皮	皮	皮	皮					

chǐ	尸							ㄱ コ 尸 尺 (4)
尺	尺	尺	尺					

kuài	土							一 十 土 圵 圵 块 块 (7)
块	块	块	块					

bǎ	扌							一 寸 扌 扌 扣 扣 把 (7)
把	把	把	把					

jiā	大							一 ㇐ 口 ㅛ 夹 夹 (6)
夹	夹	夹	夹					

bō	扌				一 寸 扌 扌 扩 护 抨 抨 採 採 播 播 播 (15)
播	播	播	播		

qì	口			㇑ 宀 口 叮 叩 吅 吅 咢 哭 哭 哭 器 器 器 器 (16)
器	器	器	器	

4.4 网上词典
Online Dictionaries

一. LISTENING PRACTICE

I. Phrase Dictation. Listen carefully to Audio Clip 4-4-1. Each phrase will be read twice, first at normal speed for you to get a general idea, and then at slow speed for you to write down the phrase in pinyin.

1. _____

2. _____

3. _____

4. _____

5. _____

6. _____

II. Sentence Dictation. Listen carefully to Audio Clip 4-4-2. Each sentence will be read twice, first at normal speed for you to get a general idea, and then at slow speed for you to write down the sentence in pinyin.

1. _____

2. _____

3. _____

4. _____

5. _____

III. Listen carefully to Audio Clip 4-4-3 and then place tone marks above each character in the poem.

小 时 不 识 月，呼 作 白 玉 盘。

又 疑 瑶 台 镜，飞 在 青 云 端。

IV. Listen to Dialogue 1 from Lesson 4.4 and then answer the True/False questions in Audio Clip 4-4-4.

	1	2	3	4	5
对					
错					

V. Listen to Dialogue 2 from Lesson 4.4 and then answer the True/False questions in Audio Clip 4-4-5.

	1	2	3
对			
错			

VI. Listen to the students talking about their opinions about online dictionaries in Audio Clip 4-4-6. Draw lines to indicate 1) if this person likes to use online dictionaries and 2) why.

谁   喜欢不喜欢   为什么

1. 大卫   _____   不喜欢用电脑。

2. 汤姆   喜欢用   挺聪明的，我不用词典。

3. 凯丽   _____   非常容易用。

4. 玛丽娅   不喜欢用   不常常上网。

5. 杰米   _____   用起来很方便。

VII. Listen to Audio Clip 4-4-7 and write down what each person is dissatisfied with.

1. 第一个人：_____

2. 第二个人：_____

3. 第三个人：_____

4. 第四个人：_____

5. 第五个人：_____

6. 第六个人：_____

VIII. Listen carefully to the questions in Audio Clip 4-4-8 and write your answers in complete sentences.

1. _____

2. _____

3. _____

4. _____

5. _____

二. 综合语言练习 INTEGRATED LANGUAGE PRACTICE

I. How do you say it in Chinese?

Section 1: Phrases

1. online dictionary

_____

2. chat online

_____

3. easy to use

_____

4. movie DVD

_____

5. to store files

_____

6. history book

_____

7. very convenient

_____

8. world history

_____

9. like the most

_____

10. computer files

_____

Section 2: Sentences

1. Why don't you use a USB flash drive?

_____

2. An MP3 player is very easy to use.

_____

3. I heard that many people in China play computer games online.

_____

4. Do you have the web address?

_____

5. I've got this book on CD.

_____

6. An USB drive is used to store computer files.

_____

7. I use my MP3 player to listen to music and to store computer files.

_____

8. Look, there are so many history books: American history, Chinese history, the world history, and (even) history of computers.

_____

II. Pair Activity: What Are These Things?

Step 1: Draw lines to match the questions in Column A with the answers in Column B. Don't let your partner see your answers, as the two of you will compare your answers later to see how many correct answers each person gets.

Column A	Column B
1. 什么是"优盘"?	a. 那是上课用的书。
2. 什么是"MP3播放器"?	b. 那是在互联网上看书、看电影什么的。
3. 什么是"DVD光盘"?	c. 那是存电影用的光盘。
4. 什么是"蜡笔"?	d. 那是画画儿用的彩色笔。
5. 什么是"练习本"?	e. 那是放书和文具用的包。
6. 什么是"书包"?	g. 那是查生词和生词用的书。
7. 什么是"课本"?	h. 那是存电脑文件用的,非常小的东西。
8. 什么是"词典"?	i. 那是一个网页在互联网上的地址。
9. 什么是"上网"?	j. 那是存和播放音乐的小机器。
10. 什么是"网站"?	k. 那是写作业用的本子。

Word Bank

互联网	hùliánwǎng	World Wide Web

Step 2: Now take turns with your partner to ask each other questions in Column A. Listen carefully to your partner's answer and compare it with yours. In the table below, record the number of correct answers that your partner gets.

	1	2	3	4	5	6	7	8	9	10
对										
不对										

III. **Small Group Activity: My Favorite Things**

Step 1: You would like to get to know your classmates better. Find three people that you don't know very well and form of group of four. First fill out the sheet below for yourself, and then talk to two other students.

我是谁?

* * * * * * * * * *

我最喜欢的

书 _____

课 _____

人 _____

动物 _____

颜色 _____

运动 _____

活动 _____

音乐 _____

电影 _____

电视 _____

我的名字是 _____

Step 2: Interview your partner and fill out the information card below for him/her.

你是谁？

* * * * * * * * * *

你最喜欢的

书 _____

课 _____

人 _____

动物 _____

颜色 _____

运动 _____

活动 _____

音乐 _____

电影 _____

电视 _____

你的名字是 _____

Step 3: Now talk to a third classmate in your group and interview him/her about what he/she has found out about his/her partner.

他/她是谁？

*　*　*　*　*　*　*　*　*　*

他/她最喜欢的

书 _____

课 _____

人 _____

动物 _____

颜色 _____

运动 _____

活动 _____

音乐 _____

电影 _____

电视 _____

他/她的名字是 _____

IV. Scrambled Sentences

Put the following sentences in correct order based on the clues given in English.

1. 有 很多 电影 现在 和 网上 音乐。

_____

(There are lots of movies and music on the Internet nowadays.)

2. 文件 光盘 这 有 张 很多 音乐 上。

_____

(There are many music files on this CD.)

3. 很多 听说 用 现在 优盘 人 文件 存放。

_____

(I hear that many people now use USB flash drives to store documents.)

4. 听 MP3 非常 音乐 用 方便 播放器。

_____

(It is very convenient to listen to music using MP3 player.)

5. 借 托尼 电脑，我 的 用用，你 好 吗?

_____

(Tony, may I borrow your computer?)

6. 支 的 不 是 这 红，是 笔 的 黄。

_____

(This pen is not red. It's yellow.)

V. **Pair Activity: May I Borrow...**

Step 1: Circle seven items from the pictures below. Don't let your partner see your choices, because later he/she will try to borrow them from you. The items that you've circled are what you have in your backpack. The rest of the items are what you'd like to borrow from your partner.

1.	2.	3.	4.
5.	6.	7.	8.
9.	10.	11.	12.

Step 2: Enter the names of the items that you wish to borrow in the form below, and then ask your partner if you may borrow them. Place a check mark next to the items that you have successfully borrowed.

Model: **A:** 借你的铅笔用用，好吗？

   B: 好。你用吧。 **or** 对不起，我也没有铅笔。

你要借的东西 **The things you'd like to borrow:**

Item	√	Item	√
1.		2.	
3.		4.	
5.		6.	
7.		8.	
9.		10.	

VI. Pair Activity: Learn from You

你：   你朋友：

1A:	You start first. You see your classmate holding a little white box with earphones extending out. You are curious to learn what it is.	**1B:**	You are holding an iPod in your hand. Your classmate is curious and would like to know what it is.

你：哎，这是什么？

你：iPod? 是小电脑吗？

你：这叫iPod。

你：好啊！(Listen ...) 哇，真好听！这个iPod可以存多少个歌？

你：不是。iPod 和MP3播放器一样，是存音乐的。你要不要听听？

你：那么多！哎，这个iPod可以和MP3一样存汉字文件吗？

你：要看文件大小。差不多200多个。

你：太好了。我也要买一个。

你：可以，我就用iPod存我的汉语练习和中国音乐。

你朋友：   你：

2A: Your classmate would like to borrow your Chinese folk music CD. Instead of lending it to him/her, tell him/her that it is actually available online for free.	2B: You start first. You would like to borrow your friend's Chinese folk music CD. Then you learn that the music is freely available online.
你：好啊，可是你为什么不上网听呢？	你：哎，借我你的中国音乐光盘听听，好吗？
你：有啊！你可以免费下载。	你：网上有吗？
你：在 www.chinesemusic.com。	你：真的？在哪个网站？
你：是啊，上网听音乐非常方便。有喜欢的音乐，你就可以存在你的电脑上。	你：太好了！你常常在网上免费下载音乐吗？
	你：太好了。我今天晚上回家试试。

Word Bank

1. 哇 wà wow	2. 免费下载 miǎnfèi xiàzài free download; download for free	3. 歌 gē song
4. 可以 kěyí may, be able to	5. 试试 shìshi give it a try	

VII. Match Them!

Match the characters in Column A with pinyin pronunciations in Column B and English meanings in Column C.

Column A	Column B	Column C
词典	tīngshuō	give, to
网上	chángcháng	world
网站	shàngwǎng	a measure word
容易	zhāng	USB flash drive
方便	fāngbiàn	dictionary
听说	cídiǎn	CD, DVD disk
常常	wǎngshàng	go online
上网	wǎngzhàn	online
世界	yōupán	it is said
光盘	gěi	convenient
给	róngyì	website
张	guāngpán	floppy diskette
优盘	shìjiè	often
存文件	cún wénjiàn	store/save file
磁盘	cípán	easy

三. 汉字练习   CHINESE CHARACTER PRACTICE

姓名：_____

I. Write the characters in the correct stroke order.

cí	讠								丶 讠 订 订 词 词 词 (7)
词	词	词	词						

diǎn	八								丨 冂 日 曲 曲 典 典 (8)
典	典	典	典						

zhàn	立								丶 亠 六 六 立 站 站 站 站 站 (10)
站	站	站	站						

róng	宀								丶 宀 宀 宀 宀 宀 容 容 容 容 (10)
容	容	容	容						

yì	日								丨 冂 日 日 月 号 易 易 (8)
易	易	易	易						

biàn	亻								丿 亻 亻 亻 伫 佰 佰 便 便 (9)
便	便	便	便						

tīng	口								丨 冂 口 叮 听 听 听 (7)
听	听	听	听						

shuō	讠								丶 讠 讠 讠 讱 说 说 说 说 (9)
说	说	说	说						

shì	一								一 十 卅 卅 世 (5)
世	世	世	世						

jiè	田								丨 冂 日 田 田 罗 界 界 界 (9)
界	界	界	界						

zuì	日	丨 冂 冂 日 旦 甼 具 冐 骨 最 最 最 (12)
最 最 最 最		

guāng	儿	丨 丨 丨 业 业 光 (6)
光 光 光 光		

pán	皿	丿 丿 丿 月 舟 舟 舟 舟 盘 盘 (11)
盘 盘 盘 盘		

gěi	纟	乚 纟 纟 纟 纠 纠 给 给 给 (9)
给 给 给 给		

zhāng	弓	丁 丁 弓 弘 弘 张 张 (7)
张 张 张 张		

yōu	亻	丿 亻 仁 什 优 优 (6)
优 优 优 优		

cún	子	一 ナ 才 存 存 存 (6)
存 存 存 存		

cí	石	一 丆 丆 石 石 石 矿 矿 磁 磁 磁 磁 磁 磁 (14)
磁 磁 磁 磁		

4.5 我带滑板
I Will Take a Skateboard

一．听力练习 LISTENING PRACTICE

I. Phrase Dictation

Listen carefully to Audio Clip 4-5-1. Each phrase will be read twice, first at normal speed for you to get a general idea, and then at slow speed for you to write down the phrase in pinyin.

1. _____

2. _____

3. _____

4. _____

5. _____

II. Sentence Dictation

Listen carefully to Audio Clip 4-5-2. Each sentence will be read twice, first at normal speed for you to get a general idea, and then at slow speed for you to write down the sentence in pinyin.

1. _____

2. _____

3. _____

4. _____

5. _____

III. Listen carefully to Audio Clip 4-5-3 and then place tone marks above each character in the poem.

篱 落 疏 疏 一 径 深，树 头 花 落 未 成 荫。

儿 童 急 走 追 黄 蝶，飞 入 菜 花 无 处 寻。

IV. Listen to Dialogue 1 from Lesson 4.5 and then answer the True/False questions in Audio Clip 4-5-4.

	1	2	3	4	5
对					
错					

V. Listen to Dialogue 2 from Lesson 4.5 and then answer the True/False questions in Audio Clip 4-5-5.

	1	2	3	4
对				
错				

VI. Rejoinders: What would be the most appropriate responses to the questions you hear in Audio Clip 4-5-6? Circle the correct answers from the choice below.

Question 1

A. 对不起。我有事。

B. 看电影以后我们打球吧。

C. 好，我也带一个。

Question 2

A. 带，老虎和我们一队。

B. 好吧，那我带一些纸巾。

C. 不要带东西。

Question 3

A. 怎么打篮球？

B. 我们喜欢溜旱冰和打篮球！

C. 好，你有篮球吗？

Question 4

A. 他最喜欢看你溜旱冰。

B. 我喜欢玩滑板。

C. 打篮球以后我们去溜旱冰。

Question 5

A. 他们有两个篮球。

B. 你有足球吗？

C. 大卫玩滑板，我们溜旱冰。

VII. What to Take?

The Mandarin Club is planning a picnic in the park next weekend. What do they need to bring? Listen carefully to what the club president says in Audio Clip 4-5-7 and circle the items that she has mentioned from the list below.

汉语俱乐部野餐要带的东西 Things to Take to the Mandarin Club Picnic					
篮球	足球	网球	滑板	旱冰鞋	刀叉
盘子	杯子	纸巾	红笔	蜡笔	汉堡
可口可乐	热狗	面包	咖啡	蛋糕	冰淇淋

二. 综合语言练习　INTEGRATED LANGUAGE PRACTICE

I. How do you say it in Chinese?

Section 1: Phrases

1. two soccer balls

_____

2. three basketballs

_____

3. one tennis ball

_____

4. two forks

_____

5. some cups

_____

6. six plates

_____

7. one knife

_____

8. paper napkins

_____

9. a pair of rollerblades

_____

10. a skateboard

_____

Section 2: Sentences

1. Let's play basketball.

_____

2. How about we play soccer before the picnic?

_____

3. How would you like to go shopping after dinner?

_____

4. Let's go to a movie after class.

_____

5. Let's go to my house to play video games.

_____

II. Pair Activity: What Shall We Do?

Student A

Your Mandarin study group will meet this Friday afternoon from 3:00-4:00 to review for the upcoming unit test. Someone in the group proposed that, if it's possible, all of you go to a new Chinese movie before or after the meeting. But it seems that most group members have other engagements for the afternoon already. Using the chart below, find out what each person plans to do before and after the meeting.

Step 1: In the column marked 你, write down what you plan to do.

Step 2: Ask your partner what he/she plans to do and record the answers in the column marked 你朋友。

Step 3: Ask your partner what other people (in the pictures) plan to do.

Model: **A:** 你学习以前做什么？
　　　　　　B: 我看电影。你呢？

　　　　　　A: 小弟学习以后做什么，你知道吗？
　　　　　　B: 他学习以后看电视。

	你	你朋友	大明	小弟	小虎	小林
学习以前						
学习以后						

Student B

Your Mandarin study group will meet this Friday afternoon from 3:00-4:00 to review for the upcoming unit test. Someone in the group proposed that, if it's possible, all of you go to a new Chinese movie before or after the meeting. But it seems that most group members have other engagements for the afternoon already. Using the chart below, find out what each person plans to do before and after the meeting.

Step 1: In the column marked 你, write down what you plan to do.

Step 2: Ask your partner what he/she plans to do and record the answers in the column marked 你朋友。

Step 3: Ask your partner what other people (in the pictures) plan to do.

Model:　**A:** 你学习以前做什么？
　　　　　B: 我看电影。你呢？

　　　　　A: 大明学习以后做什么，你知道吗？
　　　　　B: 他学习以后打网球。

	你	你朋友	大明	小弟	小虎	小林
学习以前						
学习以后						

III. Group Activity: Let's Go to a Picnic!

You and some friends are going to have a picnic this weekend. Get together with your friends and follow the steps below to discuss who will bring which item to the picnic.

Step 1: Select a group leader, whose job is to enter the discussion results in the list below.

Step 2: On the list, circle two items that you intend to bring, but do not let your friends see your choices.

Step 3: Your group leader will ask who'd like to bring each item. Answer the leader's questions based on your choices. But if someone else plans to bring the same thing, you will have to negotiate with this person or choose to bring something else on the list.

Group leader: As the leader you will have to do the following two things: 1) Ask who'd like to bring each item, and 2) record the answers on the list.

Model:

Leader: 谁要带篮球？

Member 1: 我有篮球，我带吧。

Member 2: 你要带篮球吗？那我带纸巾吧。

野餐要带的东西 **Things to Take to the Picnic**	
谁带？	物品名称
	汉堡包（8个）
	热狗（10个）
	可乐（四瓶）
	纸巾（两包）
	杯子（20个）
	盘子（20个）
	刀叉（各20把）
	足球（1个）

IV. Write a Note

Write short notes to your friends based on the scenarios; each note should be about 50 words, including punctuation.

1. Write a note to Tom, asking if he would like to join you and other friends to a picnic this Sunday afternoon. Tell him to call you tonight and let you know of his decision.

2. Write a note to Kelly, asking her to bring her rollerblades and a basketball to the park this Saturday.

3. Write a note to Mary, asking her if she would like to play soccer with you and some friends this afternoon. Tell Mary that you've heard she likes to play soccer, and invite her to be on your team.

V. Pair Activity: Let's Celebrate!

Activity 1: You will turn 15 this weekend. Your parents will host a birthday party for you and ask you to invite some friends over to your party. Complete the invitation dialogue, using the suggested expressions. When you finish, switch roles with your partner.

学生一： **You start first.**　　　　学生二：

你： Ask if s/he is free this Saturday, using the 是不是 form of question.	你： Confirm.
你： Invite him/her to your birthday party, using 吧 to make a suggestion.	你： Express your joy using 太 ⋯ 了. Ask how old your friend will be.
你： Tell him/her that you will be 15.	你： Ask what kind of gifts you could bring to your friend.
你： Tell him/her that a music CD would be great.	你： Agree to give your friend what he/she wants. Ask where and when the party will be held.
你： Tell him/her that the party will be at 4:30 at the People's Park.	你： Ask what your friend will be doing after the party.
你： Tell him/her that you don't have any plans yet.	你： Invite your friend to go rollerblading with you.
你： Express your joy using 太 ⋯⋯ Tell him/her you love rollerblading, using 最.	你： Remind your friend to bring a pair of rollerblades on Saturday.
你： Confirm.	你： Tell your friend that you'll see him/her on Saturday at the park.
你： Say goodbye.	

Activity 2: To welcome some new students who have recently transferred to your school, you will host a picnic party this weekend and would like to invite your friends to the party. Complete the invitation dialogue, using the suggested expressions. When you finish, switch roles with your partner.

学生一：   学生二： **You start first**

你： Confirm.	你： Ask your friend if he is free this Sunday afternoon, using 是不是 type of question.
你： Agree. Ask who else will be at the picnic.	你： Invite him/her to come to your picnic, using 好吗? type of tag questions.
你： Express your excitement, using 太···了! Ask where and when the party will be held.	你： Tell him/her that many Chinese students will be there and that he/she can practice Chinese.
你： Ask what you may bring to the picnic.	你： Tell him/her it will be held on Sunday at 1 at the Golden Gate Park.
你： Agree. Tell your friend that you will bring four Chinese music CDs with you. Ask what people will do before the picnic.	你： Tell him/her that you heard that he/she has some Chinese music CDs and ask if he/she could bring a few to the picnic.
你： Tell your friend that soccer is your favorite sport, using 最.	你： Tell him/her that you will play soccer before the picnic. Ask if he/she likes to play soccer.
你： Agree. Ask what your friend plans to do after the picnic.	你： Overjoyed. Ask him/her to join your team.
你： Ask if your friend and his/her Chinese guests would like to join you to a Chinese movie.	你： Tell him/her that you don't know yet.

你： Agree. Say goodbye.	你： Express your interest, but indicate that you'll have to ask your Chinese friends about it.

VI. **Put the following scrambled sentences in correct order, based on the English clues.**

1. 星期天 滑板 人民公园 玩 我们 去，好吗？

_____

(Let's go skateboarding at the People's Park this Sunday.)

2. 野餐 踢 汤姆 和 以前 玛丽 足球 要。

_____

(Tom and Mary are going to play soccer before the picnic.)

3. 以后 打 玩 溜 篮球，你们 旱冰，我。好吧，滑板

_____

(OK, you will rollerblade while I skateboard after we play basketball.)

4. 我们 再 是 买 两 双 不是 旱冰鞋 星期六？

_____

(Should we buy two more pairs of rollerblades this Saturday?)

5. 星期六 你 生日 知道 是 妈妈 的 不知道

_____

(Do you know that mom's birthday is this Saturday?)

VII. Character Bingo

Follow the instructions for Character Bingo in Lesson 4.2.

Word Bank

磁盘	光盘	播放器	优盘	盘子
刀叉	杯子	旱冰鞋	野餐	踢足球
溜旱冰	打篮球	带东西	滑板	纸巾
词典	上网	网站	方便	容易

Bingo Grid

VIII. Match Them!

Match the characters in Column A with pinyin pronunciations in Column B and English meanings in Column C.

Column A	Column B	Column C
打球	pánzi	picnic
踢足球	liū huábǎn	pair (a measure word)
篮球队	bēizi	before
旱冰鞋	yěcān	paper napkin
双	shuāng	cup
溜滑板	dāochā	rollerblades
野餐	dǎqiú	plate
杯子	zhǐjīn	play ball
盘子	yǐqián	basketball team
刀叉	lánqiúduì	also, again
纸巾	tī zúqiú	play football
再	zài	knife and fork
以前	hànbīng xié	skate on a skateboard

三. 汉字练习 CHINESE CHARACTER PRACTICE

姓名：＿＿＿＿＿＿＿＿＿＿＿＿

I. Write the characters in the correct stroke order.

a	口	丶 丨 口 叮 叮 叮 䀹 啊 啊 (10)
啊	啊 啊 啊	
zú	足	丶 口 口 口 尸 尸 足 (7)
足	足 足 足	
lán	竹	ノ 𠂊 𠂇 𥫗 𥫗 竺 筥 筥 筥 筥 筥 篁 篁 篮 篮 篮 (16)
篮	篮 篮 篮	
liū	氵	丶 冫 氵 氵 氵 汈 汈 汈 溜 溜 溜 溜 溜 (13)
溜	溜 溜 溜	
hàn	日	丶 口 口 日 旦 旱 旱 (7)
旱	旱 旱 旱	
bīng	冫	丶 冫 冫 冫 冰 冰 (6)
冰	冰 冰 冰	
xié	革	一 十 廾 廿 廿 革 革 革 革 鞋 鞋 鞋 鞋 鞋 鞋 (15)
鞋	鞋 鞋 鞋	
shuāng	又	丁 又 双 双 (4)
双	双 双 双	
huá	氵	丶 冫 氵 氵 汩 汩 汩 汩 汩 滑 滑 滑 (12)
滑	滑 滑 滑	
bǎn	木	一 十 才 木 杚 杦 板 板 (8)
板	板 板 板	

| yě | 里 | 丨 口 曰 日 甲 甲 里 野 野 野 野 (11) |
| 野 | 野 野 野 | |

| cān | 食 | ′ ヘ ゲ ゲ ゲ 夕 夗 夗 奴 癶 夻 夻 夻 夻 夻 餐 餐 (16) |
| 餐 | 餐 餐 餐 | |

| bēi | 木 | 一 十 才 木 朾 朾 杯 杯 (8) |
| 杯 | 杯 杯 杯 | |

| dāo | 刀 | フ 刀 (2) |
| 刀 | 刀 刀 刀 | |

| chā | 又 | フ 又 叉 (3) |
| 叉 | 叉 叉 叉 | |

| zhǐ | 纟 | ∠ ∠ 纟 纟 纤 纤 纸 (7) |
| 纸 | 纸 纸 纸 | |

| jīn | 巾 | 丨 冂 巾 (3) |
| 巾 | 巾 巾 巾 | |

| qián | 刂 | ′ ″ 并 并 前 前 前 前 前 (9) |
| 前 | 前 前 前 | |

| tī | 足 | 丨 冂 口 口 足 足 足 趴 趴 趴 趴 踢 踢 踢 (15) |
| 踢 | 踢 踢 踢 | |

| duì | 阝 | 了 阝 队 队 (4) |
| 队 | 队 队 队 | |

4.6 第四单元复习
Review of Unit 4

综合语言练习   INTEGRATED LANGUAGE PRACTICE

I. First recite the poem by following Audio Clip 4-6-1, and then write a poem in Chinese about your favorite season.

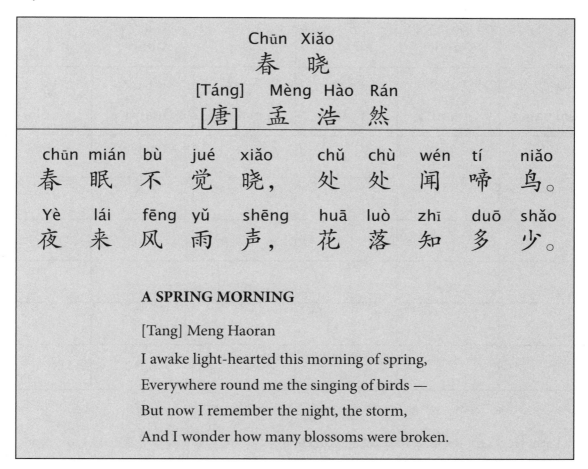

Chūn Xiǎo
春　晓

[Táng]　Mèng Hào Rán
[唐]　孟　浩　然

chūn mián bù jué xiǎo   chǔ chù wén tí niǎo
春　眠　不　觉　晓，　处　处　闻　啼　鸟。

Yè lái fēng yǔ shēng huā luò zhī duō shǎo
夜　来　风　雨　声，　花　落　知　多　少。

A SPRING MORNING

[Tang] Meng Haoran

I awake light-hearted this morning of spring,

Everywhere round me the singing of birds —

But now I remember the night, the storm,

And I wonder how many blossoms were broken.

II. Pair Activity: Donating School Supplies

In order to help children from remote areas of China to have a basic education, you and your friend are donating a backpack full of school supplies to the Hope Project every month.

Cultural Note: The Hope Project（希望工程）was established to help poor children receive a basic education. Some children from poor families, particularly those in remote and less developed rural areas in China, are unable to go to school because of financial constraints. Some rural schools also need learning materials. Through donated money and other resources, the Hope Project helps not only individual students but also schools.

Discuss with your friend what you'd like to include in this month's backpack. On a separate sheet of paper, draw an open backpack and fill it with the study materials that you'd like to donate. Then, fill out the donation form, indicating the names, quantity and color of the items that you have included in the backpack.

捐献物品单 **Donation List**					
捐献人： **Donor:**			捐献人： **Donor:**		
名称 **Item name**	数量 **Quantity**	颜色 **Color**	名称 **Item name**	数量 **Quantity**	颜色 **Color**

III. Interview and Report: Market Research

Suppose you are doing your summer internship at a marketing company. You are asked to conduct an Internet user survey. Your task is to interview at least five students on their Internet surfing behavior, and then write a report based on your interviews.

Step 1: Walk around the classroom and interview one student at a time. Ask him/her the following questions and record the answers in the interview form.

	学生一	学生二	学生三	学生四	学生五
你每天上网吗？					
你在学校还是在家上网？					
你家用宽带上网还是电话上网？					
你最喜欢上网做什么？					
你常常去的网站是哪个？					
你常常在网上下载音乐和电影吗？					
你常常用网上词典吗？为什么？					
你喜欢去网上聊天吗？为什么？					

Word Bank

聊天	liáotiān	chat

Step 2: Based on your findings, write a report about students' Internet surfing behavior.

学生上网调查

报告人：_____

_____

_____

_____

_____

_____

_____

_____

_____

_____

_____

_____

_____

_____

_____

_____

_____

_____

_____

_____

_____

IV. Board Game: Name That Character

After throwing the dice, read out the character that you land on. If you cannot recognize the character, you may use a question mark to ask a friend for help. Every player has two "question marks" to start with. If you are lucky, you may collect more question marks in the game. Once you have used up your question marks, you cannot get help from your friends anymore. If a player cannot recognize the character and is out of question marks, s/he is out of the game.

以	踢	球	叉	?	园	纸	刀	野	Finish
🔺	双	溜	餐	把	巾	杯	还	前	块
队	史	世	容	?	存	张	文	给	🔺
🔺	易	?	界	典	站	便	买	黄	夹
词	网	方	大	铅	件	笔	见	光	🔺
🔺	鞋	滑	篮	蓝	?	板	公	冰	Start

你有两个 "??"

V. Write the character in the correct stroke order.

| kuān 宀 | 丶丷宀宁宁审审审宽宽 (10) |

宽 宽 宽 宽

第五单元 娱乐活动

UNIT 5 Recreational Activities

5.1 看电影
Seeing a Movie

一. 听力练习 LISTENING PRACTICE

I. Phrase Dictation. Listen carefully to Audio Clip 5-1-1. Each phrase will be read twice, first at normal speed for you to get a general idea, and then at slow speed for you to write down the phrase in pinyin.

1. _____

2. _____

3. _____

4. _____

5. _____

II. Sentence Dictation. Listen carefully to Audio Clip 5-1-2. Each sentence will be read twice, first at normal speed for you to get a general idea, and then at slow speed for you to write down the sentence in pinyin.

1. _____

2. _____

3. _____

4. _____

5. _____

III. Listen carefully to Audio Clip 5-1-3 and then place tone marks above each character in the poem.

少 小 离 家 老 大 回，乡 音 未 改 鬓 毛 衰。

儿 童 相 见 不 相 识，笑 问 客 从 何 处 来。

IV. Listen to the recording of Dialogue 1 from Lesson 5.1 first, and then answer the True/False questions in Audio Clip 5-1-4.

	1	2	3	4	5
对					
错					

V. Listen to the recording of Dialogue 2 from Lesson 5.1 first, and then answer the True/False questions in Audio Clip 5-1-5.

	1	2	3	4
对				
错				

VI. Mary, Tom, Tony and Linda are talking about their weekend plans. Listen to Audio Clip 5-1-6 and find out what each person would like to do. Please place a check mark under the activities that each person plans to do in the table below.

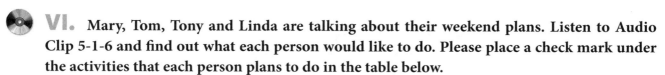

玛丽							
汤姆							
托尼							
林达							

VII. Rejoinders: What would be the most appropriate responses to the questions you hear in Audio Clip 5-1-7? Choose the correct answers from the choices below.

Question 1:

A. 嗯，我看看我有没有事。

B. 看电影以后我们打球吧。

C. 好，我可以带一个篮球。

Question 2:

A. 你要在家做作业。

B. 好吧，那我带一些本子。

C. 几点去?

Question 3:

A. 怎么打篮球?

B. 我喜欢野餐!

C. 怎么都可以。

Question 4:

A. 哎呀，我现在没有时间。

B. 对不起，我不想看书。

C. 好啊，看什么电影?

Question 5:

A. 哦，我想先看电影，再打篮球。

B. 哦，我要先去书店买一本书。

C. 哦，电影的名字是《木兰》。

二. 综合语言练习 INTEGRATED LANGUAGE PRACTICE

I. Read aloud the poem while following Audio Clip 5-1-8. Pay special attention to your tones. Afterwards, use the same title to write a poem of your own and then share it with your classmates.

Wǒ Xiǎng, Wǒ Xiǎng

我 想，我 想

Wǒ xiǎng zuò yī zhī xiǎo niǎo, yōu rán de zài tiān kōng fēi xiáng.

我 想 做一只小鸟， 悠 然地在天 空 飞 翔。

Wǒ yào zuò yī tiáo xiǎo hé, jìng jìng de zài shān jiān liú tǎng.

我 要 做一条 小河， 静 静地在 山 间 流淌。

Wǒ kě yǐ zuò yī piàn sēn lín, qiāo qiāo de gěi dà dì chuān shàng lǜ zhuāng.

我 可以做一片 森林， 悄 悄 地给大 地 穿 上 绿 装。

Wǒ màn màn de zhēng kāi yǎn jīng, bǎ yuàn wàng dōu xiě zài zhǐ shàng.

我 慢 慢 地 睁 开眼睛，把 愿 望 都 写 在 纸 上。

I wish to be a bird that flies freely in the sky.

I want to be a river that flowes peacefully in the hills.

Or I can be a forest that dresses the Earth with green.

Slowly, I open my eyes, and write down my wishes.

New Words

小鸟	xiǎoniǎo	small bird
悠然地	yōuránde	carefree and leisurely, long, distant, far away
天空	tiānkōng	the sky, the heavens
飞翔	fēixiáng	circle in the air, hover
河	hé	river
静静地	jìngjìngde	quietly
山间	shānjiān	in the mountains

流淌	liútǎng	flow, drip, shed, trickle
片	piàn	measure word for forest
森林	sēnlín	forest
悄悄地	qiāoqiāode	quietly
大地	dàdì	earth, mother earth
穿上	chuānshàng	to put on, to wear, to be dressed in
绿	lǜ	green
装	zhuāng	attire, outfit, clothing
慢慢地	mànmànde	slowly, gradually
睁开	zhēngkāi	open (the eyes)
眼睛	yǎnjing	eye
愿望	yuànwàng	desire, wish, aspiration

‖ **How do you say it in Chinese?**

1. I'd like to see a movie tonight.

_____

2. Would you like to go along?

_____

3. Could I play basketball?

_____

4. Would you give me some money?

_____

5. Let's have dinner first, and then go to a movie.

_____

6. I can take you to dinner tomorrow evening.

_____

7. You may not go to the movie with us.

_____

8. I'd like to go, too.

_____

9. Shall we see the 8 o'clock movie?

_____

10. Go early and come back on time.

_____

III. Pair Activity: Summer Camp Rules

A's Sheet

You are interested in attending a summer language camp（夏令营）in Beijing, and you decide to give the camp office a call to find out the activities and rules at the camp.

Step 1: Read through the table below and make sure you recognize all the characters.

Step 2: Ask your partner, who plays the role of the camp counselor, if you are able to do the following activities at the camp.

Model: 请问，在夏令营我们能打篮球吗？

Step 3: Listen carefully to your partner's answer and check the appropriate boxes in the table.

Step 4: Switch roles with your partner.

Word Bank

1. 夏令营 xiàlìngyíng summer camp	2. 上街 shàngjiē to go out to the street

你想做的活动	能	不能
打篮球		
踢足球		
溜旱冰		
说英语		
上街买书		
看英语电影		
吃中国饭		
上网下载音乐		

B's Sheet

You are one of the counselors at a summer language camp（夏令营）in Beijing, China. Today you received a phone call from a prospective student, asking what kind of activities students can do at the camp.

Step 1: Read through the table below and make sure you recognize all the characters.

Step 2: Decide which activities are allowed at the camp. Please think carefully before making your rules!

Step 3: Listen carefully to your partner's questions and answer them according to your rules.

Model: （你同伴）:请问，在夏令营我们能打篮球吗？

（你）:对不起，你们不能打篮球。or 当然能打篮球。

Step 4: Switch roles with your partner.

Word Bank

1. 夏令营 xiàlìngyíng summer camp	2. 上街 shàngjiē to go out to the street

活动	能	不能
打篮球		
踢足球		
溜旱冰		
说英语		
上街买书		
看英语电影		
吃中国饭		
上网下载音乐		

IV. Pair Activity: The New Rules for the School Library

A's Sheet

Imagine that you are the head librarian at your school. Today you are reviewing the library rules. Your job is to decide what a student can or cannot do in the library and why, as you will have to justify your decision to your school principal (played by your partner) later.

Step 1: Examine the following activities, make your decisions and indicate the reasons for your decisions in the appropriate columns.

活动	可以	不可以	为什么？
做作业			
吃东西			
睡觉			
用电脑			
看书			
说话			

Step 2: Report your decisions to your school principal. You must use complete sentences.

Model: A: 在图书馆可以吃东西吗？

B: 在图书馆不可以吃东西，因为……

Word Bank

图书馆	túshūguǎn	library

Step 3: Switch roles with your partner.

B's Sheet

Imagine that you are the principal of your school. Today the head librarian at your school (played by your partner) will update you on new rules regarding the use of the library.

Step 1: Read the following table and make sure you know all the characters in the first column.

Step 2: Ask your partner what his/her decision is. Listen carefully to your partner's report and record the librarian's decisions in the form below.

Model: A: 在图书馆可以吃东西吗？

B: 在图书馆不可以吃东西，因为……

活动	可以	不可以	为什么？
做作业			
吃东西			
睡觉			
用电脑			
看书			
说话			

Word Bank

图书馆	túshūguǎn	library

Step 3. Switch roles with your partner.

V. Pair Activity: Freshmen P.E. Classes

A's Sheet

Imagine that you are the principal of your school. Today the athletic director of your school (played by your partner) will update you on the P.E. course offerings to the freshmen class. Listen carefully to your partner's report and indicate his/her decisions and justification for those decisions in the form given below.

课程	可以	不可以	为什么?
篮球课			
足球课			
游泳课			
滑雪课			
瑜伽课			
武术课			

Word Bank

1. 瑜伽 yújiā yoga	2. 武术 wǔshù martial arts

B's Sheet

Imagine that you are the athletic director of your school. Today you will report to your school principal (played by your partner) which P.E. classes a freshman may or may not take next year. You also need to justify your decisions.

Step 1: Examine the following activities and indicate your decisions and the reasons for your decisions in the appropriate columns.

课程	可以	不可以	为什么？
篮球课			
足球课			
游泳课			
滑雪课			
瑜伽课			
武术课			

Word Bank

1. 瑜伽 yújiā yoga	2. 武术 wǔshù martial arts

Step 2: Report your decision to the principal for approval. You must use complete sentences.

Model: 我想，一年级的学生可以上足球课，因为…

VI. **Pair Activity: Going out with a Friend**

A's Sheet

Step 1: Do you know how to say the following sentences in Chinese? Please write down your answers either in pinyin or in characters.

1. Are you free this Friday afternoon?

_____

2. Would you like to play basketball with me?

_____

3. Don't worry. We can do homework together first, and then play basketball.

_____

4. What time would be good for you? (When do you have free time?)

_____

5. How about 2:30?

_____

6. See you on Friday at 2:30, then?

_____

7. I'm free.

_____

8. But I need to do homework first.

_____

Step 2: Invite your friend to go out with you according to the suggestions given below.

1. Ask your friend if he is free this Friday afternoon.

_____

2. Invite your friend to play basketball with you.

_____

3. Tell your friend that you can do homework together first before playing basketball.

_____

4. Decide what time to meet (2:30 p.m., for example).

_____

5. Say goodbye (See you on Friday at 2:30!)

_____

Step 3: Switch roles. Now, your friend will invite you to go out with him/her. Listen and answer his/her questions according to the suggestions given below.

1. Tell your friend that you are free.

_____

2. Accept the invitation, but mention that you'll have to do homework first.

_____

3. Agree with your friend's proposal.

_____

4. Agree upon a time to meet.

_____

5. Say goodbye.

_____

B's Sheet

Step 1: Do you know how to say the following sentences in Chinese? Please write down your answers either in pinyin or in characters.

1. Are you free this Saturday evening?

_____

2. Would you like to watch football with me?

_____

3. Don't worry. We can do homework together first, and then watch football.

_____

4. What time would be good for you? (When do you have free time?)

_____

5. How about 5:30?

_____

6. See you on Saturday at 5:30, then?

_____

7. I'm free.

_____

8. But I need to do homework first.

_____

Step 2: Listen to and answer your friend's questions according to the suggestions given below.

1. Tell your friend that you are free.

_____

2. Accept the invitation, but mention that you'll have to do homework first.

_____

3. Agree with your friend's proposal.

_____

4. Agree upon a time to meet.

_____

5. Say goodbye.

_____

Step 3: Switch roles. Now it's your turn to invite your friend to go out with you according to the suggestions given below.

1. Ask your friend if he is free this Saturday evening.

_____

2. Invite your friend to watch football with you.

_____

3. Tell your friend that you can do homework together first before watching football.

_____

4. Decide what time to meet (5:30 p.m., for example).

_____

5. Say goodbye (See you on Saturday at 5:30!)

_____

VII. Small Group Activity: Hosting Exchange Students from Taiwan

Three exchange students from Taiwan need to find host families for two weeks while visiting your local schools. Form a group of six and decide amongst yourselves which three people will be the exchange students and which three will be the host families.

Step 1: The exchange students: Fill out the Host Family Request Form with your information and the activities that you wish your host family would allow you to do.

The host families: Fill out the Host Family Information Form with your information and house rules.

Step 2: The exchange students present themselves and their preferences for the host families.

Model: 我叫小明。我今年十五岁。这是我要去的家庭：这个家庭要喜欢运动，因为我很喜欢运动。在这个家庭里孩子可以打球，看电影，看电视，玩电子游戏，但是不要做家务⋯

Step 3: Each host family "adopts" one exchange student if there is a good match. If there isn't a perfect match, the host family and the exchange student should negotiate terms that are acceptable for both parties.

Model: 我看小明来我家很好。因为我家的人都喜欢运动。我们常常去打球，游泳，溜滑板，什么的。我家有三个孩子，两个男的，一个女的，你们可以一起运动。但是在我家不可以玩电子游戏。你看可以吗？

Host Family Request Form

(To be completed by the exchange students)

姓名：	年龄：	性别：
你想去找什么样的家庭？		
1. 这个家庭喜欢做的活动：		
2. 在这个家庭可以做的活动：		
3. 在这个家庭不可以做的活动：		

Word Bank

1. 姓名 xìngmíng full name	2. 年龄 niánlíng age	3. 性别 xìngbié gender	4. 活动 huódòng activity

Host Family Information Form

(To be completed by the host families)

姓名：	有几个孩子？	孩子的性别：

你想找什么样的学生？

1. 学生要喜欢做下面的活动：

2. 学生在家里可以做的活动：

3. 学生在家里不可以做的活动：

Word Bank

1. 姓名 xìngmíng full name	2. 年龄 niánlíng age	3. 性别 xìngbié gender	4. 活动 huódòng activity

VIII. Match Them!

Match the words in Column A with the pinyin terms in Column B and their English translations in Column C.

Column A	Column B	Column C
想	cái	may
美丽	xiān...zài...	hour
能	xiǎng	do not have free time
再说	zàishuō	first...then...
因为	xiǎoshí	because
可以	měilì	would like to, want, intend
钱	néng	only
才	méikòngr	have the ability to, can
先...再...	qián	moreover, furthermore
没空儿	yīnwèi	money
小时	kěyǐ	beautiful

IX. Character Bingo

Follow the instructions for Character Bingo in Unit 4.2.

Word Bank

想	美丽	能	再说	因为
可以	上海	钱	幼儿园	才
先	再	晚	小时	早
没空儿	电影	做作业	书店	睡觉

Bingo Grid

X. **Put the scrambled sentences into correct order, based on the English clues.**

1. 星期天 想 滑板 人民公园 玩 我们 去。

_____

(We'd like to go skateboarding at the People's Park this Sunday.)

2. 野餐 踢 汤姆 先 足球 要 再。

_____

(Tom wants to play soccer first, and then have the picnic.)

3. 看 可以 我们 电影 晚上 八点 的 吗?

_____

(Could we see the eight o'clock movie tonight?)

4. 爸爸，你 去 我 带 可以 买 旱冰鞋 星期六 一双 吗?

_____

(Dad, could you take me to buy a pair of rollerblades this Saturday?)

5. 幼儿园 你 这个 是 电影 看 的，不能。

_____

(You are in kindergarten and may not see this movie.)

三. 汉字练习 CHINESE CHARACTER PRACTICE

姓名：_____

1. Write the characters in the correct stroke order.

xiǎng 心	一 十 才 木 村 扣 相 相 相 相 想 想 想 (13)	
想 想 想 想		
lì 一	一 丁 厅 而 丽 丽 丽 (7)	
丽 丽 丽 丽		
néng 月	ㄥ ㄙ 台 台 育 育 育 能 能 能 (10)	
能 能 能 能		
kòng 宀	丶 丷 宀 宀 穴 宓 空 空 (8)	
空 空 空 空		
qián 钅	丿 𠂉 𠂆 钅 钅 钅 钅 钱 钱 钱 (10)	
钱 钱 钱 钱		
cái 一	一 十 才 (3)	
才 才 才 才		
xiān 儿	丿 𠂉 牛 生 先 先 (6)	
先 先 先 先		

5.2 音乐
Music

一. 听力练习 **LISTENING PRACTICE**

I. Phrase Dictation. Listen carefully to Audio Clip 5-2-1. Each phrase will be read twice, first at normal speed for you to get a general idea, and then at slow speed for you to write down the phrase in pinyin.

1._____

2._____

3._____

4._____

5._____

II. Sentence Dictation. Listen carefully to Audio Clip 5-2-2. Each sentence will be read twice, first at normal speed for you to get a general idea, and then at slow speed for you to write down the sentence in pinyin.

1._____

2._____

3._____

4._____

5._____

III. Listen carefully to Audio Clip 5-2-3 and then place tone marks above each character in the poem.

泠 泠 七 弦 上，静 听 《松 风》 寒。

古 调 虽 自 爱，今 人 不 多 弹。

IV. Listen to Dialogue 1 from Lesson 5.2 and then answer the True/False questions in Audio Clip 5-2-4.

	1	2	3	4	5
对					
错					

 V. Listen to Dialogue 2 from Lesson 5.2 and then answer the True/False questions in Audio Clip 5-2-5.

	1	2	3	4
对				
错				

 VI. Listen carefully to Audio Clip 5-2-6 and find out what Mary, Tom, Tony, Linda, Nina and Mike are doing. Check the appropriate activities in the table below.

玛丽						
汤姆						
托尼						
琳达						
妮娜						
迈克						

VII. Rejoinders: What would be the most appropriate responses to the parts of dialogues you hear in Audio Clip 5-2-7? Choose the correct answers from the choices below.

Dialogue 1:

A. 嗯，我今天没事。

B. 看电视以后我们打球吧。

C. 没有，你呢？

Dialogue 2:

A. 谁说的？

B. 哪里, 哪里！

C. 真的吗？

Dialogue 3:

A. 去音乐网。

B. 为什么不买 CD 呢？

C. 我只下载我喜欢的音乐。

Dialogue 4:

A. 你会弹钢琴吗？

B. 她会弹钢琴吗？

C. 我只会弹吉他。

Dialogue 5:

A. 哦，我下载音乐。

B. 哦，我喜欢听U2。

C. 哦，我不听音乐。

二. 综合语言练习　INTEGRATED LANGUAGE PRACTICE

1. Listen to the traditional folk song in Audio Clip 5-2-8. Read the lyrics aloud, paying special attention to your tones. Afterwards, translate one of your favorite songs into Chinese and share it with your classmates.

Kāng Dìng Qíng Gē

康　定　情　歌★

Pǎo mǎ liū liū de shān shàng, yī duǒ liū liū de yún yō,

跑 马 溜 溜 的 山 上,一 朵 溜 溜 的 云 哟,

Duān duān liū liū de zhào zài kāng dìng liū liū de chéng yō.

端 端 溜 溜 的 照 在 康 定 溜 溜 的 城 哟。

Yuè liang wān wān, kāng dìng liū liū de chéng yō.

月 亮 弯 弯,康 定 溜 溜 的 城 哟。

Lǐ jiā liū liū de dà jiě, rén cái liū liū de hǎo yō,

李 家 溜 溜 的 大 姐,人 才 溜 溜 的 好 哟,

Zhāng jiā liū liū de dà gē, kàn shang liū liū de tā yō.

张 家 溜 溜 的 大 哥,看 上 溜 溜 的 她 哟。

Yuè liang wān wān, kàn shang liū liū de tā yō.

月 亮 弯 弯,看 上 溜 溜 的 她 哟。

Yī lái liū liū de kàn shang rén cái liū liū de hǎo yō,

一 来 溜 溜 的 看 上 人 才 溜 溜 的 好 哟,

Èr lái liū liū de kàn shang huì dāng liū liū de jiā yō.

二 来 溜 溜 的 看 上 会 当 溜 溜 的 家 哟。

Yuè liang wān wān, huì dāng liū liū de jiā yō.

月 亮 弯 弯,会 当 溜 溜 的 家 哟。

Shì jiān liū liū de nǚ zi, rèn nǐ liū liū de ài yō,

世 间 溜 溜 的 女 子,任 你 溜 溜 的 爱 哟,

Shì jiān liū liū de nán zi, rèn nǐ liū liū de qiú yō.

世 间 溜 溜 的 男 子,任 你 溜 溜 的 求 哟。

Yuè liang wān wān, rèn nǐ liū liū de ài yō.

月 亮 弯 弯,任 你 溜 溜 的 爱 哟。

On the Paoma mountain top is a piece of cloud that shines upon Kangding City.

Crescent moon, crescent moon (over) Kangding City.

Li family's daughter is very pretty; Zhang family's son falls in love with her.

Crescent moon, crescent moon. He falls in love with her.

First he loves her beauty, second he loves her good household skills.

Crescent moon, crescent moon. She has good household skills.

All the girls in the world are yours to love; all the boys of the world are yours to pursue.

Crescent moon, crescent moon. They are all yours to love.

New Words

康定	Kāngdìng	name of a place in Sichuan Province in China
情歌	qínggē	love song
跑马山	Pǎomǎshān	Paoma Mountain in Kangding City
朵	duǒ	measure word for a cloud
云	yún	cloud
呦	yōu	a mood particle
端端	duāduān	upright, straight
照	zhào	shine, light up
城	chéng	city, town
月亮	yuèliang	the moon
弯	wān	curved, bent
人才	réncái	a person of ability, talent, (informal) handsome appearance
看上	kànshang	take a fancy to, settle on
当家	dāngjiā	manage (household) affairs

*The Kangding Love Song is a popular folk song in China. The exact origin of this song is unclear, except that it is from Kangding City of Ganze Tibetan Autonomous County in Sichuan Province. The lyrics suggest that it might be sung during the annual horse racing festival held at the Paoma Hill in Kangding. During this festival, young men and women get together and court each other.

II. How do you say it in Chinese?

Write down your answers or use an audio recorder to record your answers.

1. I'm downloading a game from the Internet.

_____

2. What are you doing?

_____

3. Are you watching TV?

_____

4. Do you know how to play the violin?

_____

5. The Chinese team and American team are having a match now.

_____

6. The teacher asked me to participate in this competition.

_____

7. She is listening to music while doing homework.

_____

8. You cannot eat while talking.

_____

9. What is your favorite computer game?

_____

10. Why didn't you buy the CD?

_____

III. Pair Activity: What Can You Do?

A's Sheet

Step 1: Study the activities in Section 1 of your worksheet to make sure that you know how to say them in Chinese. Then, circle those sports that you know how to do, but don't let your partner see your selections.

Step 2: Listen to your partner's questions and answer according to your selections. You need to answer the questions in complete sentences.

Model: (你的同学：) 你会打篮球吗？

(你：) 我不会打篮球。

Section 1

Step 3: Study the activities in Section 2 of your worksheet to make sure that you know how to say them in Chinese. Then ask if your partner knows how to do the activities in Section 2. Circle his/her answers.

Section 2

B's Sheet

Step 1: Study the activities in Section 1 of your worksheet to make sure that you know how to say them in Chinese. Then, ask your partner if he/she knows how to do each of the activities depicted. Circle his/her answer.

Model: (你：) 你会打篮球吗？
(你的同学：) 我不会打篮球。

Section 1

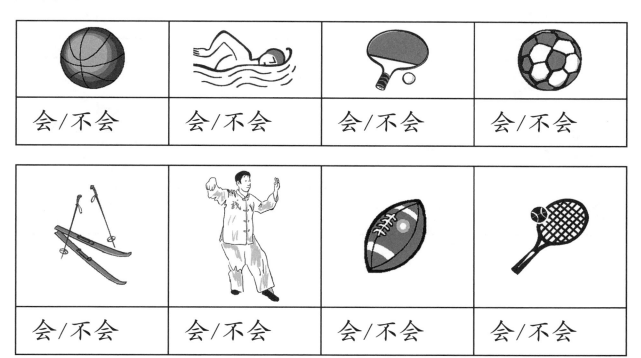

Step 2: Study the activities in Section 2 of your worksheet to make sure that you know how to say them in Chinese. Then, circle those activities that you know how to do, but don't let your partner see your selections.

Step 3: Listen to your partner's questions and answer according to your selections. You need to answer the questions in complete sentences.

Section 2

IV. Pair Activity: What Are They Doing?

Fill in the missing information in your chart by asking your partner questions, such as: 大卫正在做什么？or 大卫做什么呢？ When you finish, both you and your partner should have activities checked off for each person.

A's Sheet

	打电话	吃东西	上课	打球	睡觉	下载游戏	下载音乐	看电影	弹吉他	拉小提琴
大卫 Dàwèi					√					
小明 Xiǎomíng										
林芳 Lín Fāng										√
约翰 Yuēhàn										
马丁 Mǎdīng			√							
珍妮 Zhēnní										
林达 Líndá						√				
黛安 Dài'ān										
玛丽 Mǎlì	√									
马克 Mǎkè										

B's Sheet

	打电话	吃东西	上课	打球	睡觉	下载游戏	下载音乐	看电影	弹吉他	拉小提琴
大卫 Dàwèi										
小明 Xiǎomíng								√		
林芳 Lín Fāng										
约翰 Yuēhàn		√								
马丁 Mǎdīng										
珍妮 Zhēnní				√						
林达 Líndá										
黛安 Dài'ān							√			
玛丽 Mǎlì										
马克 Mǎkè									√	

V. Group Activity: Name That Celebrity

Step 1: Work individually. Think of a celebrity and write a description of him/her in the information form that your teacher will pass out to you. An extra copy of the form is included here for you to practice.

Step 2: Get together in groups of five students. Try to complete all the sentences in each person's information form.

Step 3: Fold the form twice and drop it into a box that your teacher has prepared for your group.

Step 4: Exchange your box with another group.

Step 5: Randomly pick a folded form from the box and have one person read it aloud – except for the last line – to your group. After you finish reading, ask your group: 他/她是谁? Your group members must guess who is being described. If after four tries nobody can guess it correctly, you can tell them the answer.

他/她是谁?

****

他/她最喜欢的人是 _____

他/她养的动物是 _____

他/她最喜欢的颜色是 _____

他/她最喜欢做的运动是 _____

他/她唱的歌是 _____

他/她演的电影是 _____

他/她写的书是 _____

他/她的名字是 _____

Word Bank

演	yǎn	to perform

VI. Pair Activity: Small Talk

Step 1: How do you say the following sentences in Chinese?

1. Hello! (when answering the phone)

_____

2. What are you doing?

_____

3. Are you doing homework, too?

_____

4. Would you like to play tennis this afternoon?

_____

5. Which website do you go to in order to download games?

_____

6. I can lend you my CD.

_____

7. I am doing homework while downloading music from the Internet.

_____

8. Let's meet at my house at 4 o'clock.

_____

9. See you at 4!

_____

10. Great!

_____

Step 2: Now have a conversation using the expressions you wrote down in Step 1.

Student A: You start.	**Student B: Your partner starts.**
1. Call B and ask what he/she is doing. Wait for the reply. 2. Tell B that you don't have any homework. You are listening to music while playing a game. 3. Tell B that you are playing Dynasty Warriors. 4. Ask B if he/she'd like to come over tomorrow afternoon. 5. Say goodbye.	1. Greet A, and tell A that you are doing Mandarin homework. Ask if A has any homework. 2. Ask A which game he/she is playing. 3. Tell A that you love that game too, and that you can play together some time. 4. Agree. Tell A that you will be there at 3 o'clock. 5. Say goodbye.

Student A: Your partner starts.	**Student B: You start.**
1. Tell B that you are watching a soccer match between the French team and the British team. Ask B if he/she is watching TV. 2. Ask from which website B downloads his music. 3. Tell B that you don't know how to play tennis. 4. Express happiness. Ask B when and where to meet. 5. Agree. Say goodbye.	1. Call A and ask what he/she is doing. 2. Tell A that you are not watching TV. You are downloading music from the Internet. 3. Tell A that you use iTunes® music store. Ask A if he/she would like to play tennis tomorrow. 4. Tell A that you can teach him/her. 5. Tell A that you can meet at the school tomorrow at 2. 6. Say goodbye.

VII.   Match Them!

Match the words in Column A with the pinyin terms in Column B and the English translations in Column C.

Column A	Column B	Column C
歌	zhèng	an adverb indicating an action in progress
竖琴	Fǎguó	(sports) match, competition
比赛	shùqín	France
正	gē	harp
球赛	bǐsài	know how to play the violin
一边···一边···	qiúsài	download
弹吉他	xiàzài	ball game
下载	yībiān... yībiān...	song
法国	huì xiǎotíqín	play guitar
会小提琴	lā dàtíqín	(doing two things) simultaneously
拉大提琴	tán jítā	play the cello

VI. Character Bingo

Follow the instructions for Character Bingo in Unit 4.2.

Word Bank

法国	正	比赛	球赛	下载
歌	弹	拉	会	能
小提琴	竖琴	大提琴	钢琴	吉他
一边	游戏	电脑	音乐	参加

Bingo Grid

VII. **Put the following scrambled sentences into correct order, based on the English clues.**

1. 电脑 正在 我 游戏 呢。 下载

_____

(I'm downloading a computer game.)

2. 看球， 正呢。 一边 他们 吃饭 一边

_____

(They are watching a ball game while eating.)

3. 在 下载 可以 只 我 我 的 歌。 网上， 喜欢

_____

(On the Internet I can download only those songs that I like.)

4. 这个 比赛。 学校 有 足球 晚上 星期五

_____

(There will be a soccer match at school this Friday evening.)

5. 我 是 钢琴 那 比赛 幼儿园 想 学生 的。

_____

(I think that is the piano competition by the kindergarten students.)

6. 的 老师 让 来 她 比赛 她 参加 竖琴。

_____

(Her harp teacher asked her to participate in the competition.)

7. 妈妈 拉 会 弹， 我 还 大提琴 会 钢琴。

_____

(My mom can play the piano as well as the cello.)

8. 姐姐 会 吉他 只 弹。

_____

(My sister only knows how to play guitar.)

VIII. Composition: Multi-Tasking

In the following table, write check marks in the squares next to the activities that you like to do simultaneously. Then write at least eight sentences describing yourself using 一边⋯ 一边 ⋯

Model: 我喜欢一边吃晚饭一边看电视。

	吃饭	唱歌	看电视	做作业	听音乐	用电脑	看书	运动
吃晚饭								
看电视								
听音乐								
玩电脑游戏								
上网聊天								
看书								
弹吉他								
唱歌								

_____

_____

_____

_____

_____

_____

_____

_____

_____

IX. On a separate piece of paper, write a description of the picture below using 正, 正在, or 在 to describe actions in progress. Your description must include the following information and must have a beginning, a middle and an end.

Who are they?　　　　(i.e., 这是小华的一家。)

What time is it?　　　(i.e., 现在是晚上九点二十分。)

What are they doing?　(i.e., 妈妈正在看书。)

三. 汉字练习　CHINESE CHARACTER PRACTICE

姓名：＿＿＿＿＿＿＿＿＿＿＿

I. Write the characters in the correct stroke order.

zhèng	止								一 丁 下 正 正 (5)
正	正	正	正						
bǐ	比								一 匕 比 比 (4)
比	比	比	比						

zài	车	一 十 土 圡 吉 幸 幸 载 载 载 (10)
载 载 载 载		

sài	贝	丶 丶 宀 宀 宀 审 宲 宲 寏 寏 寨 赛 赛 (14)
赛 赛 赛 赛		

gē	欠	一 一 一 一 可 可 可 哥 哥 哥 歌 歌 歌 (14)
歌 歌 歌 歌		

tán	弓	丁 弓 弓 弓 弓 弹 弹 弹 弹 弹 (11)
弹 弹 弹 弹		

lā	扌	一 十 才 扌 扩 拉 拉 拉 (8)
拉 拉 拉 拉		

tí	扌	一 十 才 扌 护 护 护 捍 捍 捍 捍 提 (12)
提 提 提 提		

qín	王	一 二 干 王 王 珏 珏 珏 珏 琴 琴 琴 (12)
琴 琴 琴 琴		

shù	立	丨 丨 丨 收 坚 竖 竖 竖 竖 (9)
竖 竖 竖 竖		

jí	口	一 十 士 吉 吉 吉 (6)
吉 吉 吉 吉		

5.3 电脑游戏
Computer Games

一. 听力练习 **LISTENING PRACTICE**

I. Phrase Dictation

Listen carefully to Audio Clip 5-3-1. Each phrase will be read twice, first at normal speed for you to get a general idea, and then at slow speed for you to write down the phrase in pinyin.

1. _____ 2. _____

3. _____ 4. _____

5. _____ 6. _____

7. _____ 8. _____

II. Sentence Dictation

Listen carefully to Audio Clip 5-3-2. Each sentence will be read twice, first at normal speed for you to get a general idea, and then at slow speed for you to write down the sentence in pinyin.

1. _____

2. _____

3. _____

4. _____

5. _____

III. Listen carefully to Audio Clip 5-3-3 and then place tone marks above each character in the poem.

千 里 黄 云 白 日 曛，北 风 吹 雁 雪 纷 纷。

莫 愁 前 路 无 知 己，天 下 谁 人 不 识 君。

IV. Listen to Dialogue 1 from Lesson 5.3. Based on Dialogue 1, answer the True/False questions in Audio Clip 5-3-4.

	1	2	3	4	5
对					
错					

V. Listen to Dialogue 2 from Lesson 5.3. Based on Dialogue 2, answer the True/False questions in Audio Clip 5-3-5.

	1	2	3	4	5
对					
错					

VI. Mary, the reporter for the school newspaper, is interviewing Maria, Tom, Tony and Jimmy about how much time they spend playing computer games every day. Listen to their conversations in Audio Clip 5-3-6 and fill out the following form.

	父母让吗?	玩几个小时?
玛丽娅		
汤姆		
托尼		
杰米		

VII. Rejoinders. What would be the most appropriate responses to the parts of dialogues you hear in Audio Clip 5-3-7? Choose the correct answers from the choices below.

Dialogue 1:

A. 在学校。

B. 不在。

C. 我是他妈妈。

Dialogue 2:

A. 我们几点去?

B. 谁说的?

C. 让我玩儿半小时。

Dialogue 3:

A. 对，我明天去。

B. 什么考试?

C. 他知道了。

Dialogue 4:

A. 我知道了。

B. 我吃了饭就做。

C. 好，等一会儿。

Dialogue 5:

A. 我们有饺子吗?

B. 我喜欢一边吃饭一边看电视。

C. 我吃了饭就去。

二. 综合语言练习 INTEGRATED LANGUAGE PRACTICE

I. **How do you say it in Chinese?**

Write down your answers or use an audio recorder to record your answers.

1. "Is Michael in?" "This is he."

_____

2. Don't you know we have a test tomorrow?

_____

3. My parents let me play for two hours.

_____

4. There is a question on page 10 that I didn't understand.

_____

5. I'll call you later.

_____

6. You should watch less TV and exercise more.

_____

7. He does homework as soon as he comes home.

_____

8. What would you like to eat tonight?

_____

9. How come you are not watching the match between China and France?

_____

10. I'll play tennis for an hour, and then go home.

_____

II. Pair Activity: How Long Is He Allowed to …?

You and your classmate are taking turns to baby-sit Tommy, your neighbor's child. Both of you know that Tommy's parents have strict rules as to how long he may spend on certain activities; yet both of you have forgotten some of the details of these rules. So you decide to get together and compare notes. When you finish, both of your charts should be completely filled out.

Model: A: 汤姆看电视可以看多久？

B: 他看电视可以看两个小时。

A's Sheet

活动 Activity	时间 Time
弹钢琴	半个小时
拉大提琴	
画画儿	二十分钟
玩电子游戏	
听音乐	
看电视	最多一个小时
上网	
学汉语	最少一个小时
运动	
看法语书	半个小时

B's Sheet

活动	时间
弹钢琴	
拉大提琴	最少四十分钟
画画儿	
玩电子游戏	最多半个小时
听音乐	二十分钟
看电视	
上网	最多一个小时
学汉语	
运动	二十分钟
看法语书	

III. **Pair Activity: You and Me**

Instructions for A

Step 1: Write down your answers to the following questions.

Step 2: Ask your partner the questions and record his/her answers.

Step 3: Listen to your partner's questions and answer them according to what you've written down.

Instructions for B

Step 1: Write down your answers to the following questions.

Step 2: Listen to your partner's questions and answer them according to what you've written down.

Step 3: Ask your partner the questions and record his/her answers.

1. 你每天运动吗?

   你：_____

   你的朋友：_____

2. 你运动几个小时?

   你：_____

   你的朋友：_____

3. 你父母让你玩儿电脑游戏吗?

   你：_____

   你的朋友：_____

4. 在家你可以上网吗?

   你：_____

   你的朋友：_____

5. 你会去哪个网站下载音乐?

   你：_____

   你的朋友：_____

6. 你每天先做作业再玩儿还是先玩儿再做作业?

   你：_____

   你的朋友：_____

7. 你每天下了课就做什么?

   你：_____

   你的朋友：_____

IV. Pair Activity: Rules of the "School for Talented Youth"

You are a student at a student-governed alternative school called the "School for Talented Youth." This year the Student Board has decided to revise its regulations on student conduct. The Board has asked the students to submit their suggestions.

Pair up with a classmate. First, each of you completes the following sentences individually. Then take turns reading your statements to each other, discussing whether you agree or disagree with each other and why.

Before you begin, there are a couple of words that you may want to use in your discussions:

Word Bank

1. 觉得 juéde feel, think	2. 同意 tóngyì agree

Model: 你：我觉得学生应该可以玩电脑游戏。
你同学：我不同意，因为学生应该学习。

	不同意	同意
我们应该＿＿＿点上课，＿＿＿点下课。	＿＿＿	＿＿＿
我们每节课应该上＿＿＿＿＿＿分钟。	＿＿＿	＿＿＿
我们中午的午饭时间应该是＿＿＿＿＿。 分钟。	＿＿＿	＿＿＿
我们上课的时候应该可以＿＿＿＿＿＿。	＿＿＿	＿＿＿
学生下课以后应该＿＿＿＿＿＿＿＿。	＿＿＿	＿＿＿
老师给学生的作业应该＿＿＿＿＿＿＿。	＿＿＿	＿＿＿
学生晚上应该＿＿＿＿＿＿＿＿＿＿。	＿＿＿	＿＿＿
学生周末的时候应该＿＿＿＿＿＿＿。	＿＿＿	＿＿＿
我们的考试应该可以＿＿＿＿＿＿＿。	＿＿＿	＿＿＿
我们的课外活动应该＿＿＿＿＿＿＿。	＿＿＿	＿＿＿

V.   Pair Activity: What's Next?

A's Sheet

Your school's scheduler, by mistake, placed your schedule in your friend's folder and your friend's schedule in your folder. Call him/her up and find out what your daily schedule is like. You must use the V1 了 O1 就 V2 O2 structure.

Model: **A:** 请告诉我，我上了中文课就上什么课？

   B: 你上了中文课就上美国历史课。

Please write your schedule in the form below.

第一节	中文课
第二节	
第三节	
第四节	
	午饭
第五节	
第六节	

Below is your friend's class schedule.

第一节	中文课
第二节	美国历史课
第三节	物理课
第四节	数学课
	午饭
第五节	经济课
第六节	英文课

B's Sheet

Your school's scheduler, by mistake, placed your schedule in your friend's folder and your friend's in your folder. Call him/her up and find out what your daily schedule is like. You must use V1 了 O1 就 V2 O2 structure.

Model: A: 请告诉我，我上了中文课就上什么课？

B: 你上了中文课就上美国历史课。

Please write your schedule in the form below.

第一节	中文课
第二节	
第三节	
第四节	
	午饭
第五节	
第六节	

Below is your friend's class schedule.

第一节	中文课
第二节	物理
第三节	数学
第四节	英文
	午饭
第五节	美国历史课
第六节	化学

VI. Find Your Soulmate

You have always believed that you have a soulmate in the midst of your classmates, and that the two of you share many things in common. Choose a set of characteristics that describe yourself, and go around the classroom to find your soulmate. Write his/her name in the space provided.

A:	B:
你们都很聪明。	你们都很聪明。
你们都会打篮球。	你们都不喜欢运动。
你们都不会弹钢琴。	你们都会拉大提琴。
你们每天都作了作业就玩电脑游戏。	你们每天都作了作业就看电视。
你们玩电子游戏都可以玩半个小时。	你们每天拉大提琴都拉四十分钟。
你们都喜欢一边吃饭一边看电视。	你们都喜欢一边听音乐一边做作业。
你们觉得考试的时候应该可以看书。	你们都觉得老师不应该给学生作业。
你们的父母都不让你们下载音乐。	你们的父母都不让你们玩电子游戏。
_____	_____

C:	D:
你们都很聪明。	你们都很聪明。
你们都不喜欢运动。	你们都会打篮球。
你们都不会弹钢琴。	你们都会拉大提琴。
你们每天都作了作业就看电视。	你们每天都作了作业就玩电脑游戏。
你们每天拉大提琴都拉四十分钟。	你们每天拉大提琴都拉四十分钟。
你们都喜欢一边吃饭一边看电视。	你们都喜欢一边吃饭一边看电视。
你们觉得考试的时候应该可以看书。	你们都觉得老师不应该给学生作业。
你们的父母都不让你们玩电子游戏。	你们的父母都不让你们看电视。

E:

你们都很聪明。

你们都会打篮球。

你们都不会弹钢琴。

你们每天都作了作业就看电视。

你们玩电子游戏都玩半个小时。

你们都喜欢一边听音乐一边做作业。

你们觉得考试的时候应该可以看书。

你们的父母都不让你们玩电子游戏。

F:

你们都很聪明。

你们都不喜欢运动。

你们都不会弹钢琴。

你们每天都作了作业就看电视。

你们玩电子游戏都可以玩半个小时。

你们都喜欢一边听音乐一边做作业。

你们都觉得老师不应该给学生作业。

你们的父母都不让你们下载音乐。

G:	H:
你们都很聪明。 你们都会打篮球。 你们都会拉大提琴。 你们每天都作了作业就玩电脑游戏。 你们玩电子游戏都可以玩半个小时。 你们都喜欢一边听音乐一边做作业。 你们都觉得老师不应该给学生作业。 你们的父母都不让你们下载音乐。	你们都很聪明。 你们都会打篮球。 你们都不会弹钢琴。 你们每天都作了作业就看电视。 你们每天拉大提琴都拉四十分钟。 你们都喜欢一边吃饭一边看电视。 你们觉得考试的时候应该可以看书。 你们的父母都不让你们下载音乐。

I:

你们都很聪明。

你们都不喜欢运动。

你们都不会弹钢琴。

你们每天都作了作业就玩电脑游戏。

你们每天拉大提琴都拉四十分钟。

你们都喜欢一边听音乐一边做作业。

你们都觉得老师不应该给学生作业。

你们的父母都不让你们下载音乐。

J:

你们都很聪明。

你们都会打篮球。

你们都不会弹钢琴。

你们每天都作了作业就看电视。

你们每天拉大提琴都拉四十分钟。

你们都喜欢一边吃饭一边看电视。

你们觉得考试的时候应该可以看书。

你们的父母都不让你们玩电子游戏。

VII. **Match Them!**

Match the words in Column A with the pinyin terms in Column B and the English translations in Column C.

Column A	Column B	Column C
考试	xià jiǎozi	cartoon
一会儿	kǎoshì	frozen, ice
父母	bīng	parents
还	yīnggāi	how come…
卡通	wǎnfàn	test, exam
应该	hái	cook dumpling
怎么	huílái	then
就	zěnme	(not) yet
晚饭	kǎtōng	return, come back
冰	fùmǔ	a little while
回来	jiù	dinner
下饺子	yīhuìr	should, ought to

VIII. Character Bingo

Follow the instructions for Character Bingo in Unit 4.2.

Word Bank

考试	一会儿	父母	还	卡通
应该	怎么	就	晚饭	饺子
冰	回来	下饺子	参加	下载
竖琴	小提琴	钢琴	吉他	大提琴

Bingo Grid

IX. Put the following scrambled sentences into correct order, based on the English clues.

1. 我 是 就 汤姆。

_____

(This is Tom.)

2. 考试 你 不 有 数学 吗 知道 明天?

_____

(Don't you know there is a math test tomorrow?)

3. 你 玩 父母 你 电脑 让 游戏 吗?

_____

(Do your parents allow you to play computer games?)

4. 每天 最多 你 小时 可以 一个 玩。

_____

(You can play for no more than an hour every day.)

5. 汤姆 了 回家 就 作业 做 每天。

_____

(Tom does his homework as soon as he gets home every day.)

6. 她 等 晚饭 回来 了 吃 就 我们。

_____

(We'll have dinner as soon as she's back.)

7. 你 电脑 应该 玩 少 游戏。

_____

(You shouldn't play so many computer games.)

8. 一个 问题 我 有 不 懂。

_____

(There is one question that I don't understand.)

X. **On a separate sheet of paper, write a paragraph about your life. The paragraph must address the following questions:**

1. What do you usually do once you get home from school?

2. Do you like multi-tasking? If yes, which activities do you do together?

3. Do you have any bad habits that you'd like to change? Write down some things that you'd like to do more or less of.

Try to use the following patterns: 1) 了…就…， 2) 一边…一边…， 3) 多 V，少 V.

三. 汉字练习　CHINESE CHARACTER PRACTICE

姓名：_____

I. Write the characters in the correct stroke order.

kǎo 考	一 十 土 耂 耂 考 (6)
shì 试	丶 讠 讠 讠 试 试 试 (8)
fù 父	丶 八 少 父 (4)
mǔ 母	乚 四 母 母 母 (5)
yīng 应	丶 广 广 广 应 应 (7)
gāi 该	丶 讠 讠 讠 讠 该 该 该 (8)
jiù 就	丶 二 六 古 古 京 京 京 就 就 (12)
jiǎo 饺	丿 饣 饣 饣 饣 饣 饣 饺 饺 (9)

5.4 旅行
Travel

一. 听力练习　LISTENING PRACTICE

I. Phrase Dictation. Listen carefully to Audio Clip 5-4-1. Each phrase will be read twice, first at normal speed for you to get a general idea, and then at slow speed for you to write down the phrase in pinyin.

1. _____
2. _____
3. _____
4. _____
5. _____

II. Sentence Dictation. Listen carefully to Audio Clip 5-4-2. Each sentence will be read twice, first at normal speed for you to get a general idea, and then at slow speed for you to write down the sentence in pinyin.

1. _____
2. _____
3. _____
4. _____
5. _____

III. Listen carefully to Audio Clip 5-4-3 and then place tone marks above each character in the poem.

朝 辞 白 帝 彩 云 间，千 里 江 陵 一 日 还。

两 岸 猿 声 啼 不 住，轻 舟 已 过 万 重 山。

IV. Listen to Dialogue 1 from Lesson 5.4, and then answer the True/False questions in Audio Clip 5-4-4.

	1	2	3	4	5
对					
错					

 V. Listen to Dialogue 2 from Lesson 5.4, and then answer the True/False questions in Audio Clip 5-4-5.

	1	2	3	4
对				
错				

VI. Maria, Tom, David and Kelly are preparing for a class picnic. Listen to the dialogue in Audio Clip 5-4-6 and draw lines linking each picnic item with the person who will be bringing it.

VII. Rejoinders: What would be the most appropriate responses to the questions you hear in Audio Clip 5-4-7? Choose the correct answers from the choices below.

Question 1:

A. 你要带东西吗？

B. 不用客气。

C. 带一些热狗，可以吗？

Question 2:

A. 我饿了。

B. 都可以。

C. 没关系。

Question 3:

A. 我也不知道。

B. 我不喜欢狗。

C. 我也是。

Question 4:

A. 听流行音乐吧。

B. 太好了。

C. 我喜欢流行音乐。

Question 5:

A. 你可以看一看吗？

B. 为什么？

C. 我随便。

二. 综合语言练习　INTEGRATED LANGUAGE PRACTICE

I. Listen to the song in Audio Clip 5-4-8. Read the lyrics aloud, paying special attention to your tones. Afterwards, think of one of your favorite songs about animals, translate it into Chinese and then share it with your classmates.

Xiǎo Bái Gē
小 白 鸽

Fēi yā fēi yā xiǎo bái gē, kě ài de xiǎo bái gē,
飞 呀 飞 呀 小 白 鸽，可 爱 的 小 白 鸽，

fēi dào dōng lái fēi dào xī, huān kuài dì chàng zhe ē.
飞 到 东 来 飞 到 西， 欢 快 地 唱 着 歌。

Duì zhe tài yáng xiào yī xiào, duì zhe bái yún shuō.
对 着 太 阳 笑 一 笑， 对 着 白 云 说。

Tīng nǎ chūn fēng jiǎng gù shì duō yā duō kuài huó.
听 那 春 风 讲 故 事 多 呀 多 快 活。

Wǒ yuàn zuò zhī xiǎo bái gē,
我 愿 做 只 小 白 鸽，

fēi dào gāo gāo de lán tiān bái yún shàng zuò yī zuò.
飞 到 高 高 的 蓝 天 白 云 上 坐 一 坐。

Kàn kàn bīn fēn de hǎo shì jiè, kāi dòng cǎi xiá chē.
看 看 缤 纷 的 好 世 界，开 动 彩 霞 车。

New Words

鸽	gē	pigeon, dove
欢快	huānkuài	cheerful and light-hearted
着	zhe	particle indicating an action in progress
太阳	tàiyáng	the sun
笑	xiào	smile, laugh

云		yún	cloud
春	风	chūnfēng	spring breeze
故	事	gùshi	story, tale
快	活	kuàihuo	happy, merry
愿		yuàn	hope, wish, desire, be willing
缤	纷	bīnfēn	(formal) in riotous profusion
世	界	shìjiè	world
开	动	kāidòng	start, set in motion
彩	霞	cǎixiá	rosy clouds

II. How do you say it in Chinese?

Write down your answers or use an audio recorder to record your answers.

1. I'd like to eat Chinese food.

_____

2. I want to drink some water.

_____

3. I would like to take some photos.

_____

4. Could you stop over there for a little while?

_____

5. Could you wait for a little while?

_____

6. Which do you prefer, classical music or popular music?

_____

7. So do I.

_____

8. I can wait for ten minutes.

_____

9. Anything will do for me.

_____

10. Look, there is a Burger King ahead.

_____

III. Mixer Activity: What are you going to bring to the picnic?

Your Chinese class will have a picnic this Saturday on the newly groomed campus lawn. Each student is asked to bring one item from each of the two categories:

1. Food Items: either one side dish or one bottle of your favorite drink to share.

shālā	hànbǎobāo	qìshuǐ	shuǐguǒ	chǎofàn	qiǎokèlì	règǒu
沙拉	汉堡包	汽水	水果	炒饭	巧克力	热狗

2. Entertainment: either one CD of your favorite music or one game to play.

CD	lánqiú	zúqiú	wǎngqiú	xiàngqí	pūkèpái	diànziyóuxì
CD	篮球	足球	网球	象棋	扑克牌	电子游戏

Step 1: Choose one item from each of the above categories and write it in the table below and state why you plan to bring this item. You must use the expression 我们...的时候可以...

Model:

带什么？	为什么？
足球	我们吃了饭可以玩。
水果	我们玩了足球可以吃。

Step 2: Circulate around the classroom and ask five classmates what they will be bringing to the picnic and why. Record their answers in the table below.

Model:

A: 玛丽娅，我们星期六要野餐，你要带什么吃的？

B: 我要带一个沙拉。我们吃汉堡的时候，可以吃。

A: 你要带什么玩儿的呢？

B: 我要带U2的CD，我们吃饭的时候可以听。

学生名字	带什么？	为什么？

IV. Pair Activity: Could You Do Me a Favor?

Take turns to ask your partner if s/he could do you a favor, using the expression 你可以V 一 V吗？ You will have to tell your partner why you are asking for the favor.

Step 1: Please write down five requests. You can write your own requests or use the suggestions below.

Requests	Reasons
1.	
2.	
3.	
4.	
5.	

Suggestions

Requests	Reasons
Take a look at your painting.	You don't know if it is good.
Wait for you for a while.	You need to finish your homework.
Stop at Burger King.	You'd like to use the restroom.
Listen to your music.	You'd like to bring it to the picnic.
Taste the salad.	You'd like to know if it tastes good.
Ask the teacher how to write your name in Chinese.	You forgot how to write it.

Step 2: Ask your partner if he/she could do you a favor, following the model.

Model: **A:** 你可以看一看我的作业吗？

B: 可以呀。怎么了？

A: 我不知道我做得对不对。

Step 3: Listen to the favor your partner asks you, and record her/his requests in the table.

Requests	Reasons

Word Bank

怎么了？	zěnme le	What's wrong? What happened? What's the matter?

V. Pair Activity: What is Your Opinion?

Imagine that you and your partner are in charge of the dorm life in a Chinese summer camp sponsored by your school. To ensure a relaxed yet orderly dorm life, the school gave you a list of dorm rules to enforce.

Word Bank

宿舍	sùshè	dormitory
大声	dàshēng	loudly
房间	fángjiān	room
同意	tóng yì	agree
不同意	bù tóng yì	disagree

Step 1: Read the current rules below and indicate in the space given whether or not you would agree with them and why.

	同意	不同意	为什么?
1. 在宿舍的时候			
不可以大声说话。	_____	_____	_____
不可以唱歌、跳舞。	_____	_____	_____
可以听音乐。	_____	_____	_____
2. 在房间里			
不可以吃东西。	_____	_____	_____
可以喝水、喝茶。	_____	_____	_____
可以玩电脑游戏。	_____	_____	_____
可以看电视。	_____	_____	_____
3. 在宿舍的电脑房			
不可以吃东西。	_____	_____	_____
不可以喝水。	_____	_____	_____
可以用电脑做作业。	_____	_____	_____
可以下载音乐和游戏。	_____	_____	_____
4. 在宿舍食堂吃饭的时候			
可以跟同学说话。	_____	_____	_____
可以听音乐。	_____	_____	_____
不可以玩电脑游戏。	_____	_____	_____

Step 2: Discuss each rule with your partner. Tell each other whether or not you agree with the rule and why. Record your partner's opinion in the chart.

1. 进宿舍的时候

   不可以大声说话。

   不可以唱歌、跳舞。

   可以听音乐。

   同意　不同意为什么?

   _____ _____ _____

   _____ _____ _____

2. 在房间里

   不可以吃东西。

   不可以打扰别人。

   可以喝水、喝茶。

   可以玩电脑游戏。

   可以看电视。

   _____ _____ _____

   _____ _____ _____

   _____ _____ _____

   _____ _____ _____

   _____ _____ _____

3. 在宿舍的电脑房

   不可以吃东西。

   不可以喝水。

   不可以睡觉。

   可以用电脑做作业。

   可以下载音乐。

   可以下载电脑游戏。

   _____ _____ _____

   _____ _____ _____

   _____ _____ _____

   _____ _____ _____

   _____ _____ _____

   _____ _____ _____

4. 在宿舍食堂吃饭的时候

   可以跟同学说话。

   可以听音乐。

   不可以玩电脑游戏。

   不可以带饭馆的饭去食堂吃。

   _____ _____ _____

   _____ _____ _____

   _____ _____ _____

   _____ _____

Step 3: Based on your discussions, write down the rules that both of you agree with as the new dorm rules.

1. 进宿舍的时候

_____

_____

_____

2. 在房间里

_____

_____

_____

3. 在宿舍的电脑房

_____

_____

_____

4. 在宿舍食堂吃饭的时候

_____

_____

_____

VI. Mini-Dialogues: What Should We Do?

Complete the following dialogues with your partner, following the instructions. Use any special expressions included in the instructions.

A	B
对话一 You start. – Ask B what he/she prefers for lunch: Chinese food or Western food. (还是) – Ask B if it is OK to go to Burger King for lunch.	对话一 Your partner starts. – Tell A that anything will do. (随便)
对话二 Your partner starts. – Tell B that you don't care. (随便) – Tell B that Chinese pop music is fine with you.	对话二 You start. – Ask A whether he/she would like to listen to classical or popular music. (还是) – Ask A if it would be allright to listen to some Chinese pop music.
对话三 You start. – Ask B if he/she could come to your birthday party this Saturday. (可以) – Act overjoyed! Tell B that when he/she comes over you can play your new video game together. (···的时候)	对话三 Your partner starts. – Tell A that you need to check the calendar. Then tell A that you are free in the morning. (看一看) – Tell A that you are looking forward to it.
对话四 Your partner starts. – Tell B that you need to think about it (想一想). Ask B the name of the movie. – Act overjoyed! Ask B what time the movie starts. – Tell B, with regret, that you have other plans on Friday night.	对话四 You start. – Ask A if he/she would like to see a movie with you. (想不想) – Tell A it will be the classical Japanese cartoon Totoro. – Tell A that it begins at 8 p.m. on Friday night, and that you can have dinner together before the movie. (以前)

VII. Match Them!

Match the words in Column A with the pinyin in Column B and the English translations in Column C.

Column A	Column B	Column C
旅行	fēngjǐng	stop
坐车	shuǐ	Chinese food
时候	fēnzhōng	anything will do; easy-going
熊猫	Xīcān	time
咪咪	gǔdiǎn	hungry
说话	xióngmāo	minute
分钟	tíng	beautiful
古典	shíhòu	speak, say
流行	mī mī	panda
水	shuō huà	bathroom, washroom
停	měi	Western food
风景	Zhōngcān	travel
美	è	scenery
饿	zuòchē	meow
中餐	lǔxíng	ride in a car
西餐	cèsuǒ	classical
随便	liúxíng	water
厕所	suíbiàn	popular

VIII. Character Bingo

Follow the instructions for Character Bingo in Unit 4.2.

Word Bank

旅行	坐车	时候	熊猫	咪咪	说话
古典	流行	水	停	风景	美
饿	中餐	西餐	厕所	分钟	南京
汉堡王	音乐	喝水	照片	饭店	考试

Bingo Grid

IX. **Put the following scrambled sentences into correct order, based on the English clues.**

1. 我们 去 开车 要 北京 明天。

_____

(We are driving to Beijing tomorrow.)

2. 猫 了 你 不 高兴 就 的 上车。

_____

(Your cat becomes unhappy as soon as she gets in the car.)

3. 的 时候 喜欢 看 他 吃饭 电视。

_____

(He likes to watch TV while eating.)

4. 想 中餐 吃 还是 西餐 你？

_____

(What would you like to eat, Chinese food or Western food?)

5. 我们 可以 停 停 那儿 一 在 吗？

_____

(Could we stop for a while over there?)

6. 我们 小时 等 半 可以 个。

_____

(We can wait for half an hour.)

三. 汉字练习　CHINESE CHARACTER PRACTICE

姓名：＿＿＿＿＿＿＿＿＿＿＿＿＿

I. Write the characters in the correct stroke order.

lǚ	方					` ㇐ 亠 方 方 扩 扩 疒 旅 旅 旅 (10)
旅	旅	旅	旅			

xíng	行					㇒ 彳 彳 行 行 行 (6)
行	行	行	行			

zuò	土					㇒ 人 𠆢 𠓥 𠓫 坐 坐 (7)
坐	坐	坐	坐			

chē	车					一 ㇐ 二 车 (4)
车	车	车	车			

xióng	灬					㇜ 厶 个 台 台 台 育 育 能 能 能 能 熊 熊 (14)
熊	熊	熊	熊			

māo	犭					㇒ 犭 犭 犭 犭 犭 犷 猫 猫 猫 猫 (11)
猫	猫	猫	猫			

mī	口					丨 冂 口 口 口 叩 叩 咪 咪 (9)
咪	咪	咪	咪			

biān	辶					㇇ 力 力 边 边 (5)
边	边	边	边			

gǔ	口					一 十 十 古 古 (5)
古	古	古	古			

liú	氵					` ` 氵 氵 汸 浐 浐 浐 流 流 (10)
流	流	流	流			

shuǐ 水							) 刁 水 水 (4)			
水	水	水	水							
tíng 亻						/ 亻 亻 亻 广 扩 佇 佇 停 停 停 (11)				
停	停	停	停							
fēng 风							) 几 凤 风 (4)			
风	风	风	风							
jǐng 日						丶 口 日 日 旦 旦 昌 暑 景 景 景 (12)				
景	景	景	景							
è 饣						/ ᄼ ᄾ 饣 饣 饣 饫 饿 饿 饿 (10)				
饿	饿	饿	饿							
xī 西							一 冂 冂 丙 西 西 (6)			
西	西	西	西							
suí 阝						⻖ 阝 阝 阶 阼 阽 隋 隋 隋 随 (11)				
随	随	随	随							
cè 厂							一 厂 厂 厂 厕 厕 厕 厕 (8)			
厕	厕	厕	厕							
děng 竹						/ ᄼ ᄾ 竹 竹 竹 笁 竺 竺 等 等 等 (12)				
等	等	等	等							
zhōng 钅						/ ᄼ ᄾ 生 生 钅 钅 钔 钟 (9)				
钟	钟	钟	钟							

5.5 看电视
Watching TV

一. 听力练习 LISTENING PRACTICE

I. Phrase Dictation

Listen carefully to Audio Clip 5-5-1. Each phrase will be read twice, first at normal speed for you to get a general idea, and then at slow speed for you to write down the phrases in pinyin.

1. _____   2. _____

3. _____   4. _____

5. _____   6. _____

7. _____   8. _____

II. Sentence Dictation

Listen carefully to Audio Clip 5-5-2. Each sentence will be read twice, first at normal speed for you to get a general idea, and then at slow speed for you to write down the sentences in pinyin.

1. _____

2. _____

3. _____

4. _____

5. _____

6. _____

7. _____

8. _____

III. Listen carefully to Audio Clip 5-5-3 and then place tone marks above each character in the poem.

千 山 鸟 飞 绝，万 径 人 踪 灭。

孤 舟 蓑 笠 翁，独 钓 寒 江 雪。

IV. Listen to Dialogue 1 from Lesson 5.5 and then answer the True/False questions in Audio Clip 5-5-4.

	1	2	3	4	5
对					
错					

V. Listen to Dialogue 2 from Lesson 5.5 and then answer the True/False questions in Audio Clip 5-5-5.

	1	2	3	4
对				
错				

VI. Suppose you have a brother, Anthony. While Anthony was out, one of his friends called and left a message on your family's answering machine. Please listen to the message in Audio Clip 5-5-6 carefully and fill out the message note in Chinese.

To _____

Date _____ Time _____

While you were out

Mr/Ms _____

of _____

Area code _____ Phone _____

      □ Telephoned □ Please phone

      □ Came by to see you □ Will call again

      □ Wants to see you □ Returned your call

Message

_____

_____

_____

_____

_____

VII. **Favorite TV Programs**

Tony, a reporter for the school newspaper, is preparing a report on popular TV programs among students. He is interviewing Linda now to find out her favorite TV programs. Listen to the dialogue in Audio Clip 5-5-7 and check Linda's favorite TV programs in the table below.

林达喜欢的电视节目：

新闻节目	音乐节目	体育节目	幼儿节目	文艺节目	经济节目	旅游节目	烹调节目

VIII. Rejoinders: What would be the most appropriate responses to the questions you hear in Audio Clip 5-5-8? Choose the correct answers from the choices below.

Question 1:

A. 我不喜欢。

B. 体育和音乐节目我都喜欢。

C. 我父母不喜欢我看的节目。

Question 2:

A. 我们有体育频道，新闻频道，音乐频道，什么的。

B. 妈妈只让我看英语频道的节目。

C. 五十多个。

Question 3:

A. 哪里。我一看卡通她就说要看文艺节目。

B. 姐姐星期天常常看烹调节目。

C. 姐姐不喜欢跟我看电视。

Question 4:

A. 哎呀，我现在没有时间。

B. 我不看九频道的电视节目。

C. 最多半个小时。

Question 5:

A. 没关系。

B. 我会的。

C. 我也是。

二. 综合语言练习　INTEGRATED LANGUAGE PRACTICE

I. Read the following poem after Audio Clip 5-5-9. Pay special attention to your tones. Afterwards, use the same topic to write a poem of your own and then share it with your classmates.

<table>
<tr><td colspan="10" align="center">Chūn Tiān Zài Nǎ Lǐ
春 天 在 哪 里</td></tr>
<tr><td>Chūn</td><td>tiān</td><td>zài</td><td>nǎ</td><td>lǐ,</td><td>chūn</td><td>tiān</td><td>zài</td><td>nǎ</td><td>lǐ,</td></tr>
<tr><td>春</td><td>天</td><td>在</td><td>哪</td><td>里，</td><td>春</td><td>天</td><td>在</td><td>哪</td><td>里，</td></tr>
<tr><td>chūn</td><td>tiān</td><td>zài</td><td>nà</td><td>qīng</td><td>cuì</td><td>de</td><td>shān</td><td>lín</td><td>lǐ.</td></tr>
<tr><td>春</td><td>天</td><td>在</td><td>那</td><td>青</td><td>翠</td><td>的</td><td>山</td><td>林</td><td>里。</td></tr>
<tr><td>Zhè</td><td>lǐ</td><td>yǒu</td><td>hóng</td><td>huā,</td><td>zhè</td><td>lǐ</td><td>yǒu</td><td>lǜ</td><td>cǎo,</td></tr>
<tr><td>这</td><td>里</td><td>有</td><td>红</td><td>花，</td><td>这</td><td>里</td><td>有</td><td>绿</td><td>草，</td></tr>
<tr><td>hái</td><td>yǒu</td><td>nà</td><td>huì</td><td>chàng</td><td>gē</td><td>de</td><td>xiǎo</td><td>huáng</td><td>lí.</td></tr>
<tr><td>还</td><td>有</td><td>那</td><td>会</td><td>唱</td><td>歌</td><td>的</td><td>小</td><td>黄</td><td>鹂。</td></tr>
<tr><td>Chūn</td><td>tiān</td><td>zài</td><td>nǎ</td><td>lǐ,</td><td>chūn</td><td>tiān</td><td>zài</td><td>nǎ</td><td>lǐ,</td></tr>
<tr><td>春</td><td>天</td><td>在</td><td>哪</td><td>里，</td><td>春</td><td>天</td><td>在</td><td>哪</td><td>里，</td></tr>
<tr><td>chūn</td><td>tiān</td><td>zài</td><td>nà</td><td>xiǎo</td><td>péng</td><td>yǒu</td><td>de</td><td>yǎn</td><td>jīng</td><td>lǐ.</td></tr>
<tr><td>春</td><td>天</td><td>在</td><td>那</td><td>小</td><td>朋</td><td>友</td><td>的</td><td>眼</td><td>睛</td><td>里。</td></tr>
<tr><td>Kàn</td><td>jiàn</td><td>hóng</td><td>de</td><td>huā,</td><td>kàn</td><td>jiàn</td><td>lǜ</td><td>de</td><td>cǎo,</td></tr>
<tr><td>看</td><td>见</td><td>红</td><td>的</td><td>花，</td><td>看</td><td>见</td><td>绿</td><td>的</td><td>草，</td></tr>
<tr><td>hái</td><td>yǒu</td><td>nà</td><td>huì</td><td>chàng</td><td>gē</td><td>de</td><td>xiǎo</td><td>huáng</td><td>lí.</td></tr>
<tr><td>还</td><td>有</td><td>那</td><td>会</td><td>唱</td><td>歌</td><td>的</td><td>小</td><td>黄</td><td>鹂。</td></tr>
</table>

New Words

春天	chūntiān	spring, springtime
哪里	nǎli	where, wherever
青翠	qīngcuì	verdant, fresh and green
山林	shānlín	mountains and woods
这里	zhèlǐ	here

红花	hónghuā	red flowers
黄鹂	huánglí	oriole
眼睛	yǎnjīng	eye
看见	kànjiàn	catch sight of, see

II. How do you say it in Chinese?

Write down your answers or use an audio recorder to record your answers.

1. Which TV programs do you like?

_____

2. How many TV channels can you receive at home?

_____

3. Whenever my younger brother watches cartoons, my mom asks him to go and study.

_____

4. We'd better watch the Culture & Arts program.

_____

5. I can only play for two hours every day.

_____

6. They don't have a lot of time to watch the music program.

_____

7. Every day, my younger sister yells out that she wants to eat hamburgers.

_____

8. You should exercise more.

_____

III. **Pair Activity: What kind of TV programs do you like?**

Pair up with a classmate. First, read the following questions and write down the answers for yourself in the space marked "你". Then, ask your partner the same questions about his/her TV preferences. Record your partner's answers in the space marked "你朋友". Present what your friend's TV preferences are to the class.

1. 请问，你每天都看电视吗？
   你：
   你朋友：

2. 你家的电视可以收到几个频道？
   你：
   你朋友：

3. 你喜欢看哪些频道的电视节目？
   你：
   你朋友：

4. 你最喜欢的电视剧是哪个？
   你：
   你朋友：

5. 你小的时候最喜欢看哪个卡通片？
   你：
   你朋友：

6. 看体育节目的时候，你自己看还是跟朋友和家人一起看？
   你：
   你朋友：

IV. Small Group Activity: My Favorite TV Show

Get together in a group of four. First, fill out the questionnaire below for yourself. Afterwards, share your results with your group. The group needs to select one TV show that everybody likes to watch. Each member should give one statement about why he/she would vote for watching this show.

Step 1: Fill out the following questionnaire for yourself so you can share it with your group members later.

什么样的节目	喜欢	不喜欢	最喜欢的节目叫什么名字？在哪个频道？
新闻节目			
幼儿节目			
旅游节目			
电视剧节目			
音乐节目			
游戏节目			
体育节目			

Step 2: Every group member reads out his/her TV preferences. When one person is reading, the rest of the group should record his/her statements in the table below.

Model: 我喜欢看儿童节目。我最喜欢九频道的动画片 "Sagwa".

		新闻节目	幼儿节目	旅游节目	电视剧节目	音乐节目	游戏节目	体育节目
学生一	喜欢							
	不喜欢							
	节目名字							
学生二	喜欢							
	不喜欢							
	节目名字							
学生三	喜欢							
	不喜欢							
	节目名字							

Step 3: Vote on one show that seems to be most popular among the members of your group. Each person should write down one reason for voting the way he/she does.

我们可以看 _____， 因为 _____

_____ 。

V.   Pair Activity: What's on TV This Evening?

You and your friend decide to watch CCTV Channel 4's program together. Each of you have some information about tonight's program on CCTV. Now you are trying to compare notes to get a complete TV schedule. Work together to fill in the missing information in your program table.

Model: **A:** 你能不能告诉我，今天晚上从六点到六点半有什么节目？

　　　　　　B: 可以。今天晚上从六点到六点半是新闻节目。

A's Sheet

Here is what you know about tonight's program on CCTV 4:

时间	节目	名称
6:00 – 6:30		
	幼儿节目	动画片：汉字的历史
7:00 – 8:00	旅游节目	
8:00 – 8:10		太极拳十分钟
8:10 – 9:30	文艺节目	
9:30 – 10:00		纪录片：今日中国
	音乐节目	中学生钢琴比赛

B's Sheet

This is what you know about tonight's program on CCTV 4:

时间	节目	名称
	中央电视台新闻	
6:30 – 7:00	幼儿节目	
7:00 – 8:00		纪录片：美丽的长城
8:00 – 8:10	体育节目	
8:10 – 9:30		电影：我的父亲母亲
	经济节目	纪录片：今日中国
10:00 – 11:00	音乐节目	

VI. Pair Activity: Burglary Investigation

Suppose you and your partner are helping the Campus Security in a burglary investigation. There was a burglary in one of the dorms on campus last night from 9:30 to 10:00. After some detective work, you and your partner learned that the following ten students were at the dorm at the time when the burglary occurred. The two of you interviewed these students separately and now you are comparing notes.

   Have a conversation with your partner based on the pictures below and fill out the missing information, using V着 to indicate the accompanying action.

Model: **A:** 汤姆从九点半到十点正在做什么？
  B: 那个时候他正看着电视做作业呢。

A's Sheet

Person	Activity 1	Activity 2
妮娜		
约翰		
林达		
凯丽		
马克		
大卫		
玛丽娅		
戴安		
安东尼		
汤姆		

B's Sheet

Person	Activity 1	Activity 2
妮娜		
约翰		
林达		
凯丽		
马克		
大卫		
玛丽娅		
戴安		
安东尼		
汤姆		

VII.   Match Them!

Match the Chinese characters in Column A with the pinyin words in Column B and the English translations in Column C.

Column A	Column B	Column C
电视剧	kǎtōngpiàn	newspaper
新闻	wényì jiémù	TV drama
卡通片	zhōngyāng	news
电视台	diànshìjù	travel channel
有线电视	lǚyóu píndào	arts and culture program
喊着	pàng	TV station
文艺节目	shōudào	yelling, shouting (accompanying action)
报	yǒuxiàn diànshì	cartoon film
中央	diànshìtái	TV set
收到	xīnwén	less
电视机	hǎnzhe	fat, overweight
少	diànshìjī	cable TV
旅游频道	bào	central
胖	shǎo	receive

VIII.   Chinese Word Search

Translate the sentences/phrases below into Chinese, and then find them in the word puzzle.

Clues:

1. China Central TV Station
2. entertainment program
3. old movies
4. cable TV
5. can receive more than fifty channels
6. news channel
7. sports program
8. Japanese anime
9. economic news
10. It's better to have my own TV.
11. I can watch no more than one hour TV.
12. movie channel
13. Which TV programs do you like to watch?
14. She doesn't like the TV programs that her grandma watches.
15. I like to watch ball games.

电 哈 品 龙 意 运 城 找 只 也 以 亲 孩 开 未
影 她 不 喜 欢 奶 奶 看 的 电 视 节 目 林 老
频 冷 攻 结 目 你 此 最 威 省 玉 年 道 新 电
道 外 鱼 节 吧 因 喜 名 多 香 恩 频 低 闻 影
施 红 艺 它 半 我 药 欢 博 能 个 您 索 频 告
体 文 闻 在 灵 喜 弹 死 看 多 看 亚 派 道 防
二 育 推 界 候 欢 自 验 十 哪 九 一 项 厂 省
亚 环 节 所 功 看 际 五 烈 育 些 忍 个 达 等
灯 句 温 目 决 球 到 研 夫 伤 细 电 利 小 艺
稿 都 怪 开 听 收 英 约 开 穿 有 船 视 绝 时
通 胡 志 价 以 中 央 电 视 台 院 线 换 节 订
势 责 经 可 图 皇 怀 日 视 卡 通 片 电 向 目
世 具 济 最 好 有 我 自 本 的 电 视 视 视 守
纸 微 新 告 哥 统 七 己 异 心 让 苦 机 罪 图
的 说 闻 共 印 样 怕 异 职 软 近 亮 带 跑 见

IX. **Put the following scrambled sentences into correct order, based on the English clues.**

1. 喜欢 我 旅游 看 最 节目。

_____

(I like to watch travel programs most.)

2. 我们 电脑 一 最好 看 我，人 一 有 台。

_____

(I think it's better if each of us has his own computer.)

3. 看 体育 我 一 频道，经济 她 频道 喊 要 就 着 看 的。

_____

(Whenever I watch the sports channel, she insists on watching the economic channel.)

4. 他们 有线 订 家 电视，收到 节目 的 频道 五十 可以 多 个。

_____

(His family subscribes to cable services and can receive TV programs from more than fifty channels.)

5. 我 看 电视 每天 都，看 时间 的 可是 不 长。

_____

(I watch TV every day, although not for a long time.)

X. On a separate piece of paper, write a note to your friend David, inviting him to watch the soccer game on TV with you. In your note, please include the following information:

1. Why are you writing this note to David?
2. When will the program begin?
3. Where are you going to meet?
4. How can David contact you if he can/cannot join you?

三. 汉字练习 CHINESE CHARACTER PRACTICE

姓名：_____

l. Write the characters in the correct stroke order.

mù	目							丨 冂 冂 月 目 (5)
目	目	目	目					
shì	见						`丶 ㇕ ⺀ 礻 衤 初 视 视 (8)
视	视	视	视					
jù	刂					㇕ ㇕ 尸 尺 尽 居 居 剧 剧 (10)
剧	剧	剧	剧					
wén	门					`丶 亅 门 门 闩 闩 闻 闻 闻 (9)
闻	闻	闻	闻					
yāng	大					丨 冂 冂 央 央 (5)
央	央	央	央					
tái	口					㇗ 厶 台 台 台 (5)
台	台	台	台					
yì	艹					一 十 艹 艺 (4)
艺	艺	艺	艺					

| lǚ 方 | | | | `、 ー ゙ 方 方 方 斻 斻 旅 旅 (10) | | | | | |
| 旅 | 旅 | 旅 | 旅 | | | | | | |

| hǎn 口 | | | | `丿 冂 口 叮 吖 吓 咸 咸 喊 喊 喊 (12) | | | | | |
| 喊 | 喊 | 喊 | 喊 | | | | | | |

| zhe 目 | | | | `、 丷 䒑 兰 兰 羊 羊 养 着 着 着 (11) | | | | | |
| 着 | 着 | 着 | 着 | | | | | | |

| kǎ 卜 | | | | `丿 卜 上 卡 卡 (5) | | | | | |
| 卡 | 卡 | 卡 | 卡 | | | | | | |

| tōng 辶 | | | | `マ マ 冂 肙 甬 甬 甬 涌 涌 通 (10) | | | | | |
| 通 | 通 | 通 | 通 | | | | | | |

| piàn 片 | | | | `丿 丿 尸 片 (4) | | | | | |
| 片 | 片 | 片 | 片 | | | | | | |

| bào 扌 | | | | `一 十 扌 扩 扣 担 报 (7) | | | | | |
| 报 | 报 | 报 | 报 | | | | | | |

| xiàn 纟 | | | | `乚 幺 纟 纟 纟 线 线 线 (8) | | | | | |
| 线 | 线 | 线 | 线 | | | | | | |

| shōu 攵 | | | | `乚 丩 屵 收 收 (6) | | | | | |
| 收 | 收 | 收 | 收 | | | | | | |

| pín 页 | | | | `丨 卜 扩 止 歨 歨 步 步 频 频 频 (13) | | | | | |
| 频 | 频 | 频 | 频 | | | | | | |

| pàng 月 | | | | `丿 刀 月 月 月 胖 胖 胖 胖 (9) | | | | | |
| 胖 | 胖 | 胖 | 胖 | | | | | | |

5.6 第五单元复习
Review of Unit 5

综合语言练习   INTEGRATED LANGUAGE PRACTICE

I. After reading Text 1 from Lesson 5.6, listen to the questions in Audio Clip 5-6-1. Write down the questions in pinyin as you listen, and then answer the questions in Chinese.

1. 问题：_____
   回答：_____

2. 问题：_____
   回答：_____

3. 问题：_____
   回答：_____

4. 问题：_____
   回答：_____

II. Interview: My Ideal School

Suppose your school is doing a student opinion poll on what an ideal school would be like. What should students do every day? What is the daily schedule? You are one of the poll facilitators. First write down your own opinion. Then interview three students and record their opinions in the following tables.

Word Bank

假设	jiǎshè	if, suppose

假设你有一个学校，你的学校应该什么样？＿＿＿＿＿＿＿＿

什么样的学生可以上你的学校？＿＿＿＿＿＿＿＿＿＿＿＿

学生们应该几点开始上课？＿＿＿＿＿＿＿＿＿＿＿＿＿＿

每天学生们要上几节课？＿＿＿＿＿＿＿＿＿＿＿＿＿＿＿

学生们中午可以休息一个小时吗？＿＿＿＿＿＿＿＿＿＿

下午学生们应该做运动吗？＿＿＿＿＿＿＿＿＿＿＿＿＿＿

老师要给学生们作业吗？＿＿＿＿＿＿＿＿＿＿＿＿＿＿＿

学生们在学校可以玩电脑游戏吗？＿＿＿＿＿＿＿＿＿＿

学生们可以用学校的电脑下载音乐吗？＿＿＿＿＿＿＿＿

Ask your interviewee the following questions:

第一个学生：

什么样的学生可以上你的学校？＿＿＿＿＿＿＿＿＿＿＿＿

学生们九点开始上课，可以吗？＿＿＿＿＿＿＿＿＿＿＿＿

每天学生们要上六节课吗？＿＿＿＿＿＿＿＿＿＿＿＿＿＿

学生们中午可以休息一个小时吗？＿＿＿＿＿＿＿＿＿＿

下午学生们应该做运动吗？＿＿＿＿＿＿＿＿＿＿＿＿＿＿

老师要给学生们很多作业吗？＿＿＿＿＿＿＿＿＿＿＿＿＿

学生们在学校可以玩电脑游戏吗？＿＿＿＿＿＿＿＿＿＿

学生们可以用学校的电脑下载音乐吗？＿＿＿＿＿＿＿＿

Ask the second interviewee the following questions:

第二个学生：

聪明不聪明的学生都可以上你的学校吗？＿＿＿＿＿＿＿＿＿

学生们最好几点开始上课？＿＿＿＿＿＿＿＿＿

每天学生们要上五节课还是六节课？＿＿＿＿＿＿＿＿＿

学生们中午可以休息两个小时吗？＿＿＿＿＿＿＿＿＿

下午学生们应该做什么？＿＿＿＿＿＿＿＿＿

老师要给学生们作业吗？＿＿＿＿＿＿＿＿＿

学生们在学校不可以玩电脑游戏吧？＿＿＿＿＿＿＿＿＿

学生们可以用学校的电脑下载音乐吗？＿＿＿＿＿＿＿＿＿

Ask the third interviewee the following questions:

第三个学生：

什么样的学生可以上你的学校？＿＿＿＿＿＿＿＿＿

学生们应该不应该八点开始上课？＿＿＿＿＿＿＿＿＿

每天学生们要上几节课？＿＿＿＿＿＿＿＿＿

学生们中午可以休息半个小时吗？＿＿＿＿＿＿＿＿＿

下午学生们要做运动吗？＿＿＿＿＿＿＿＿＿

老师不可以给学生们作业吧？＿＿＿＿＿＿＿＿＿

学生们在学校可以玩电脑游戏吗？＿＿＿＿＿＿＿＿＿

学生们可以用学校的电脑下载音乐吗？＿＿＿＿＿＿＿＿＿

III. **Game: Master of Translation**

After throwing the dice, answer the question in the square in Chinese. Every player has two "question marks" to start with. If you cannot answer the questions in the square in which you have landed, you may use a question mark to ask a friend for help. Once you have used up your question marks, you cannot get help from your friends anymore. If a player cannot answer the question and is out of the question marks, s/he is out of the game. The first one to reach square 25 is the master of Chinese translation!

25. **Finish**	24. 她正在做什么？（V着）	23. **Back to 10**	22. 汉语怎么说 "It would be better if I have my own TV"?	21. ◀ 汉语怎么说 "Let's ask the teacher"?
16. ▶ Skip one square	17. 汉语怎么说 "When you called I was listening to music"?	18. 汉语怎么说 "My cat is unhappy whenever he gets in a car"?	19. 玛丽正在做什么？（V着）	20. ▲ 汉语怎么说 "I am downloading music"?
15. ▲ 汉语怎么说 "She knows how to play the violin"?	14. **Go back to 3**	13. 她正在做什么？	12. 汉语怎么说 "Can we stop for lunch"?	11. ◀ 汉语怎么说 "I want to drink some water"?
6. ▶ 他正在做什么？	7. 汉语怎么说 "What would you like to eat?"	8. 汉语怎么说 "I'll do homework first, and then go to a bookstore"?	9. **Skip one square**	10. ▲ 汉语怎么说 "eating while watching TV"? （一边…一边…）
5. ▲ **Skip to 7**	4. 汉语怎么说 "You cannot watch TV today"?	3. 她正在做什么？	2. 汉语怎么说 "I'd like to see a movie tonight"?	1. **Start** ◀

IV. **You Have Mail!**

Next Monday and Tuesday morning, a group of students from the International School in Beijing is coming to visit your school. You are the chairperson of the student welcome committee. Today, you have received email from three committee members, reporting what they have planned for the guests. Suppose you will meet with the school's principal this afternoon and summarize (in English) what the student committee has planned. A blank table is provided to help you organize your summary.

Reply	Reply to All	Forward	Delete	Print	Junk	Save

下个星期二上午十点我们给北京国际学校的学生开欢迎会。我买了一些吃的和喝的东西。吃的东西有水果、饼干、和巧克力。喝的有茶、可口可乐、和水。我还应该去买一些花，所以我还要一些钱。

小明

Reply	Reply to All	Forward	Delete	Print	Junk	Save

下星期一下午两点，我们要带北京国际学校的学生去参观我们的电脑房和宿舍。汤姆和马克会在电脑房欢迎北京同学。参观电脑房以后，我们欢迎他们参加篮球比赛。球赛是下午三点开始。球赛以后，他们可以听听音乐什么的。晚上，我们可以去"熊猫饭店"吃晚饭。那儿的饺子非常好吃。

凯丽

Reply	Reply to All	Forward	Delete	Print	Junk	Save

下个星期二下午，我们可以让北京同学来参加学校的音乐会。我们学校的乐队每个星期二下午三点到五点要练习。音乐老师说，下个星期二下午，我们可以给北京的同学们开一个音乐会，乐队的学生们可以演节目。音乐会是下个星期二下午三点，在5号大楼110教室。

王丽

Monday AM	Tuesday AM
Monday PM	Tuesday PM

Word Bank

1. 开会 kāi huì to have a meeting	2. 水果 shuǐguǒ fruit	3. 饼干 bǐnggān crackers	4. 巧克力 qiǎokèlì chocolate	5. 饭店 fàndiàn restaurant

三. 汉字练习 CHINESE CHARACTER PRACTICE

姓名： _____

1. Write the characters in the correct stroke order.

yǎn	氵							`丶丶氵氵氵汴汴汴澲澲渖演演演` (14)
演	演	演	演					
chàng	口							`丨冂口口吅吅咟咟唱唱唱` (11)
唱	唱	唱	唱					
xiē	二							`丨卜止止此此些些` (8)
些	些	些	些					
chūn	日							`一二三声夫夫春春春` (9)
春	春	春	春					
jié	艹							`一十艹艻节` (5)
节	节	节	节					
bìng	疒							`丶一广广广疒疒病病病` (10)
病	病	病	病					
dú	毋							`一二十丰丰毒毒毒毒` (9)
毒	毒	毒	毒					
yùn	辶							`一二云云运运运` (7)
运	运	运	运					
ruǎn	车							`一士车车轩轩软软` (8)
软	软	软	软					

第六单元 我们生活的地方

UNIT 6 Our Environment

6.1 中国的城市
Chinese Cities

一. 听力练习 LISTENING PRACTICE

I. Phrase Dictation. Listen carefully to Audio Clip 6-1-1. Each phrase will be read twice, first at normal speed for you to get a general idea, and then at slow speed for you to write down the phrase in pinyin.

1. _____

2. _____

3. _____

4. _____

5. _____

II. Sentence Dictation. Listen to Audio Clip 6-1-2 carefully. Each sentence will be read twice, first in normal speed for you to get a general idea, and then in slow speed for you to write down the sentence in pinyin.

1. _____

2. _____

3. _____

4. _____

5. _____

6. _____

III. Listen to Audio Clip 6-1-3 carefully and underline the stressed sections.

1. 你 叫 什么 名字？

2. 他 是 汉语 老师 吗？

3. 这 是 不 是 你 的 书包？

4. 今天 是 星期五 还是 星期六？

5. 爷爷 的 生日 是 三月 四号 吗？

IV. Listen carefully to Audio Clip 6-1-4 and then place tone marks above each character in the poem.

葡 萄 美 酒 夜 光 杯，欲 饮 琵 琶 马 上 催。

醉 卧 沙 场 君 莫 笑，古 来 征 战 几 人 回？

V. Listen to the recording of the Text from Lesson 6.1 first and then answer the True/False questions in Audio Clip 6-1-5.

	1	2	3	4
对				
错				

VI. Listen to the recording of the Dialogue from Lesson 6.1 first and then answer the True/False questions in Audio Clip 6-1-6.

	1	2	3	4
对				
错				

VII. Listen carefully to the questions in Audio Clip 6-1-7 and write your answers in complete sentences in the space below.

1. _____

2. _____

3. _____

4. _____

5. _____

6. _____

7. _____

8. _____

二. 综合语言练习　INTEGRATED LANGUAGE PRACTICE

I. **How do you say it in Chinese?**

Section 1: Cities and Location Words

1. Beijing is the capital of China.

_____

2. It is in the north of China.

_____

3. There is a large city in central China.

_____

4. Shanghai is the largest city in China.

_____

5. Xi'an is an ancient city.

_____

6. Now let's turn to Southern China.

_____

7. There is a lake in the northern part of the city.

_____

8. There are many trees next to the lake.

_____

Section 2: Weekend Plans

1. What are your plans this weekend?

_____

2. Would you like to go to Xi'an?

_____

3. You can spend the weekend at my house.

_____

4. My parents will definitely be glad to meet you.

_____

5. My home is too far away (from here).

_____

6. I will go home only when we have a long weekend.

_____

7. It is two hours by train.

_____

II. Pair Activity: Complete the Maze

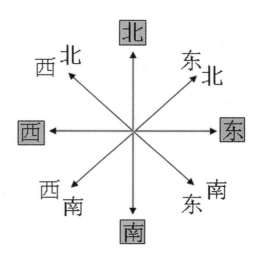

A's Sheet:

Your friend is trying to walk through the newly built maze and needs your help. S/he needs to listen to you tell her which direction to go.

Step 1: Study the route marked in black on your game board, making sure that you know how to tell directions. When your partner is ready to go, give him/her brief directions such as "东、西北、南……" until s/he successfully gets out of the maze. Remember, you can only give directions one step at a time. SWITCH! Now it is your turn to try walk-

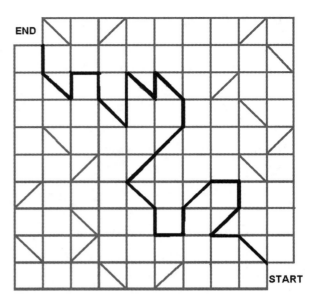

ing through the maze. Listen to your partner's directions and draw the route on the map at left.

B's Sheet:

You are going to walk through the newly built maze and need some help from your partner. Listen carefully to the directions that your partner will give you and mark the route on the map at left.

SWITCH! Now it is your partner's turn to walk

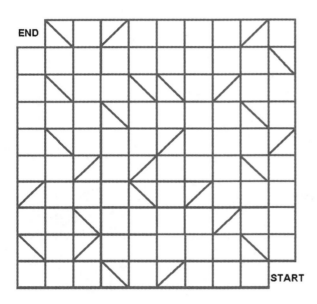

through the maze. You will be giving him/her directions.

Step 1: On your game board, select the route that you are going to tell your friend.

Step 2: When your partner is ready to go, give him/her brief directions such as "东、西北、南……"until s/he successfully gets out of the maze. Remember, your route does NOT have to be the easiest one.

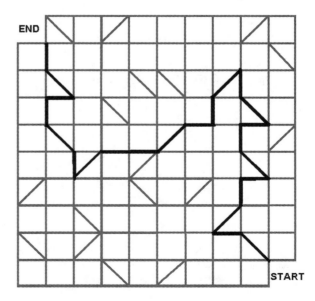

III. City Name Bingo

Step 1: Choose nine names at random from the list of the cities below and fill your game board by writing one city in each square. Make sure you know how to pronounce the cities you have chosen.

Step 2: With a partner, take turns calling each other's bingo game. Cross out each city's name as you read it. When your partner calls out a name, listen carefully, and if you have that term written in a square, cross it out with an X while telling your partner: "我有…"

Remember: you are calling your partner's bingo game and he is calling yours. The first player to cross out four terms in a row (horizontally, vertically or across) is the winner. The winner should call out: "中了！" (zhòng le).

Cities:

上海	北京	香港	杭州	旧金山
天津	西安	广州	重庆	纽约

Bingo Grid:

IV. Pair Activity: Planning a Travel Itinerary

Study your role card and complete the conversation with your partner according to the directions.

Dialogue 1

A's Card: You start first.

You are going to travel to China and would like to visit as many cities as you possibly can. You have made a tentative itinerary but are not sure if it is feasible, so you decide to call up your friend in China (played by your partner) and get some advice. Have a conversation with your partner based on the suggestions below.

1. Greet your friend on the telephone and acknowledge who you are.

_____

2. Tell your friend that you are going to China in July.

_____

3. Tell your friend that you'd like to go to Beijing first, and then to Xi'an → Chongqing → Guangzhou and then back to Beijing.

_____

4. Thank your friend for the advice. Tell him/her that you are going to travel as suggested. Ask if it is convenient for you to stay with his family.

_____

5. Act overjoyed. Say "See you in July" to your friend.

_____

B's Card: Your partner starts first.

Your friend in the United States (played by your partner) would like to travel to China. S/he has a tentative itinerary, but would like to have your opinion on how feasible the plan is. Have a phone conversation with your partner based on the suggestions given below.

1. Greet your friend on the phone, asking how s/he has been.

2. Act overjoyed to hear from your friend. Invite him/her to come see you in Beijing. Ask your friend where s/he will be traveling.

3. Tell your friend that, since Guangzhou is in southern China, Chongqing in central China, while Xi'an is in western China, it would be better to fly to Guangzhou first, then continue on to Chongqing → Xi'an → Beijing. While in Beijing your friend is welcome to stay at your house.

4. Tell your partner that your parents would love to have him/her stay for a visit.

5. Say farewell to your partner.

Dialogue 2:

A's Card: Your partner starts first.

Your friend in China (played by your partner) would like to travel to the U.S. S/he has a tentative itinerary, but would like to have your opinion on how feasible the plan is. Have a phone conversation with your partner based on the suggestions given below.

1. Greet your friend on the telephone, asking how s/he has been.

_____

2. Act overjoyed to hear from your friend. Invite your friend to come see you in New York. Ask your friend where s/he will be traveling.

_____

3. Tell your friend that, since San Francisco is in the west of the United States, New York in the east, Chicago in the north, while Las Vegas southwest, it might be better for your friend to fly to New York first, then travel to Chicago → Las Vegas → San Francisco before going home. Also invite your friend to stay with your family while in New York.

_____

4. Tell your friend that your parents would love to have him/her stay for a visit.

_____

5. Say farewell to your friend.

_____

B's card: You start first.

You are going to travel to the United States and would like to visit as many cities as you possibly can. You have made a tentative itinerary but are not sure if it is feasible. So you decide to call up your friend in the United States (played by your partner) and get some advice.

Have a conversation with your partner based on the suggestions given below.

1. Greet your friend on the telephone and acknowledge who you are.

_____

2. Tell your friend that you are going to the United States in August.

_____

3. Tell your friend that you'd like to go to San Francisco first, and then to Chicago → Las Vegas → New York, and then back to San Francisco.

_____

4. Thank your friend for the advice. Tell him/her that you are going to travel as suggested. Ask if it is convenient for you to stay with his/her family.

_____

5. Act overjoyed. Say "See you in August" to your friend.

_____

V. Group Activity: Geography Quiz

You are a member of the Geography Club at your school. At today's club meeting, you and the club members are going to have a Geography Knowledge Competition.

Step 1: Form a group of four people. Choose one person to be the group leader, who will be keeping score.

Step 2: Each member of the group (including the leader) will choose a different category from the table below, and write four questions along with their answers in the space given below. Your questions must use position words.

Model:

Regarding your neighboring countries:	哪个国家在中国的南边？
Regarding your own country:	西安在哪儿？
Regarding your own city:	北京的北边有什么？ 北京的北部有什么？
Regarding cities in China:	重庆在中国的什么地方？

Categories	Questions
你的邻国 (neighboring countries)	1. 2. 3. 4.
你的国家 (inside your own country)	1. 2. 3. 4.
你住的城市	1. 2. 3. 4.
中国的城市	1. 2. 3. 4.

Step 3: Take turns quizzing each other by reading one question from your list at a time. Note that you should finish all questions in each category before going to the next one. The person who answers the question correctly first will earn one point. Group leader: Please enter the points in the table below.

	学生一	学生二	学生三	学生四
得几分？ (Points)				
总计 (Total)				

VI. Mixer Activity: Would you Come to My Birthday Party?

To celebrate your birthday this Saturday, your parents allow you to invite your best friends over for a party. Walk around the classroom and invite three people to come to your party.

Step 1: Before inviting your friends, make sure you know the expressions used on such an occasion. For a brief review, please see the sentences in 6.1 Integrated Language Practice Activity I, Section 2. Below are some additional expressions that you may want to practice.

1. It will be my birthday on Saturday.

_____

2. We can play basketball, watch movies and play video games.

_____

3. There is a small lake next to my house. Around the lake there are many trees and flowers. It is very beautiful.

_____

4. I don't have any particular plans.

_____

5. Really? That'll be great!

_____

6. Any fun activities?

_____

7. I would love to go, but ….

_____

8. Thank you for inviting me!

_____

9. Are you sure it won't be too much trouble to your parents?

_____

Step 2: Walk around the classroom and invite three people to your party. Be enthusiastic and persuasive. Tell them how much fun it will be. Record who can attend in the space below:

The following people can attend:	
The following people cannot attend:	
The people who can attend will bring:	

When you are invited to other people's parties, be polite and kind. If you accept the invitation, ask what you will be doing at the party and if you could bring anything to the party. If you cannot make it to the party, tell people why and thank them for inviting you. You must accept one person's invitation. Please record the invitations you received and whose party you will attend in the table.

I was invited to a party by:	
I will be attending the following person's party:	
I will be bringing the following item to the party:	

VII. **Pair Activity: Commuter Survey**

You and your partner are writing an article for the school newspaper on the use of public transportation by the students to and from school. Together you have come up with a list of students whom you have interviewed. You and your partner have conducted the interviews independently. Now you are comparing notes in order to compile a complete Commuter Survey.

A's Sheet

学生的名字	家远不远？	怎么上学？	多长时间？
大卫			
玛丽娅	很远	坐火车	一个小时
凯丽			
杰米	不太远	坐地铁	半个小时
子安			
学友	挺近的	坐公共汽车	十分钟
玛丽			
妮娜	挺远的	坐地铁	四十五分钟
凯文			

Word Bank

1. 多长时间 duōcháng shíjiān how long a time	2. 近 jìn close by

B's Sheet

学生的名字	家远不远	怎么上学？	多长时间？
大卫	不太远	坐电车	十五分钟
玛丽娅			
凯丽	很近	坐地铁	十分钟
杰米			
子安	非常远	坐火车	一个半小时
学友			
玛丽	不远不近	坐公共汽车	半个小时
妮娜			
凯文	挺远的	坐火车	一个小时二十分钟

Word Bank

1. 多长时间　duōcháng shíjiān　how long a time	2. 近　jìn　close by

VIII. Match Them!

Match the characters in Column A with pinyin pronunciations in Column B and English meanings in Column C.

Column A	Column B	Column C
地图	gŭlǎo	spend
首都	zhōngbù	middle, the central part
城市	bĕibù	city
古老	shŏudū	disturb
北部	chéngshì	ancient
东南	pángbiān	side, next to
中部	dìtú	definitely
旁边	dǎrǎo	map
火车	huǒchē	West Lake
打扰	dōngnán	southeast
一定	yīdìng	capital
欢迎	huānyíng	long
远	Xīhú	train
长	guò	far
过	yuǎn	north, northern part
西湖	cháng	welcome

IX. Word Hunt

Please translate the following sentences into Chinese characters. Then find the expressions in the word puzzle.

Clues:

1. Really?
2. It won't be that way.
3. Great!
4. Sorry.
5. Never mind.
6. Thanks!
7. You are welcome.
8. Could we stop for a while?
9. Are you sure it won't be too much trouble for your parents?
10. Sorry for disturbing you.

宗	州	永	不	打	扰	你	父	母	吗
把	床	智	街	都	案	我	不	权	让
顺	没	气	爸	党	西	们	太	会	男
不	客	关	钱	上	雪	可	息	好	的
不	好	觉	系	劳	奖	以	长	陆	了
作	目	意	均	阶	样	停	血	虚	名
速	沙	易	思	众	感	一	苦	渐	的
空	对	讨	寄	打	题	停	嘴	真	英
访	不	谢	王	异	扰	吗	摘	走	刺
险	起	谢	吗	奇	载	你	卫	广	罗

X. Invitation and RSVP

Task 1. On a separate sheet of paper, write an email to your friend David, inviting him to your house this Friday to watch basketball together. Don't forget to leave your phone number so that David can call you if he has questions.

Task 2. On a separate sheet of paper, write an email response to Kelly, who has invited you to her house this weekend for her birthday party. In your email, thank Kelly for the invitation, and then tell her that you won't be able to make it because your family is taking a trip to see your grandparents. Don't forget to wish Kelly a happy birthday.

三. 汉字练习　CHINESE CHARACTER PRACTICE

姓名：＿＿＿＿＿＿＿＿＿＿＿＿

I. Write the characters in the correct stroke order.

tú	口			丨 冂 冂 冈 冈 图 图 图 (8)
图	图	图	图	
shǒu	首			丶 丷 ⺍ 产 产 首 首 首 (9)
首	首	首	首	
běi	匕			丨 ⺈ ⺈ 扌 北 (5)
北	北	北	北	
bù	阝			丶 ⺀ ⺀ 立 产 咅 音 部 部 (10)
部	部	部	部	
chéng	土			一 十 土 圫 圹 圢 城 城 城 (9)
城	城	城	城	
shì	巾			丶 亠 亠 市 市 (5)
市	市	市	市	
dōng	一			一 七 夵 东 东 (5)
东	东	东	东	
nán	十			一 十 广 冇 冇 南 南 南 南 (9)
南	南	南	南	

xiē	二							ノ ト ゖ 止 此 此 些 些 (8)
些	些	些	些				

yuǎn	辶						一 二 テ 元 元 远 远 (7)
远	远	远	远				

cháng	长						ノ 一 Ѣ 长 (4)
长	长	长	长				

huǒ	火						丶 ソ 少 火 (4)
火	火	火	火				

guò	辶						一 寸 寸 过 过 (6)
过	过	过	过				

yì	心						丶 二 ナ 立 产 音 音 音 音 意 意 意 (13)
意	意	意	意				

sī	心						ノ 口 日 田 田 甲 思 思 思 (9)
思	思	思	思				

rǎo	扌						一 十 扌 扩 扰 扰 (7)
扰	扰	扰	扰				

dìng	宀						丶 丷 宀 宁 宁 定 定 (8)
定	定	定	定				

yíng	辶						ノ ⺈ 卬 卬 卬 迎 迎 (7)
迎	迎	迎	迎				

hú	氵						丶 丶 氵 汁 沽 沽 湖 湖 湖 湖 (12)
湖	湖	湖	湖				

páng	方						丶 一 二 宀 立 产 产 㫄 旁 旁 (10)
旁	旁	旁	旁				

6.2 我们的学校
Our School

一. 听力练习 LISTENING PRACTICE

I. Dictation. Listen to Audio Clip 6-2-1 carefully. Each sentence will be read twice, first at normal speed for you to get a general idea, and then at slow speed for you to write down the sentence in pinyin.

1. _____

2. _____

3. _____

4. _____

5. _____

6. _____

II. Listen to Dialogue 1 from Lesson 6.2 first and then answer the True/False questions in Audio Clip 6-2-2.

	1	2	3	4
对				
错				

III. Listen to Dialogue 2 from Lesson 6.2 first and then answer the True/False questions in Audio Clip 6-2-3.

	1	2	3	4
对				
错				

IV. Listen to Audio Clip 6-2-4 and then place tone marks above each character in the poem.

空 山 不 见 人，但 闻 人 语 响。

返 景 入 深 林，复 照 青 苔 上。

 V. Listen to the short dialogues in Audio Clip 6-2-5 and circle the correct answers.

1. Xiao Wang

   a. likes to watch movies.

   b. went to a movie yesterday.

   c. is going to see a movie tomorrow.

2. The woman

   a. went shopping on Saturday.

   b. went skiing on Saturday.

   c. went to play basketball on Saturday.

3. The girl wanted to know

   a. if Mark brought any notebooks.

   b. if Mark is free.

   c. if Mark had erasers.

4. The man wanted to know

   a. how many books the woman borrowed.

   b. how many books the woman plans to buy.

   c. how many books the woman purchased.

5. According to the girl, her teacher

   a. went shopping yesterday.

   b. will go shopping tomorrow.

   c. is shopping now.

6. Mary

  a. didn't bring any pencils.

  b. brought two pencils.

  c. would like to borrow a pencil.

7. The man wanted to know

  a. if the woman is going to watch a soccer game tonight.

  b. if the woman watched a soccer game last night.

  c. if the woman likes to watch soccer games.

8. Mom would like to know

  a. where John went on Friday.

  b. what John will be doing this Friday.

  c. if John will be going out on Friday

VI. Listen to Nina's description of her school (Audio Clip 6-2-6) and label each building in the school plan below.

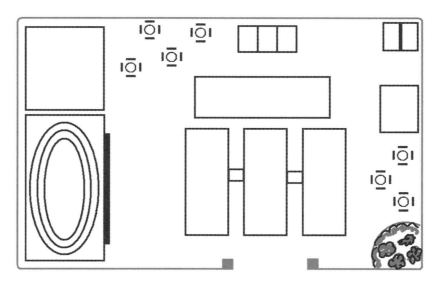

VII. Listen to the questions carefully in Audio Clip 6-2-7 and write your answers in complete sentences in the space given below.

1. _____

2. _____

3. _____

4. _____

5. _____

二． 综合语言练习   INTEGRATED LANGUAGE PRACTICE

I. How do you say it in Chinese?

Write down your answers or use an audio recorder to record your answers.

1. in front of the classroom building

_____

2. behind the sports stadium

_____

3. to the left of the cafeteria

_____

4. right of the tennis court

_____

5. outside of the library

_____

6. My school is west of Shanghai.

_____

7. The library is between the classroom building and the cafeteria.

_____

8. In front of the tennis court is our gym.

II. Pair Activity: What does your school look like?

Suppose you and your partner both attended a study abroad program in China last summer. You were studying at different schools, depicted in your worksheets below. Now you are having a chat with your partner about your school in China.

A's Sheet

Please describe your school in China to your partner. In your description, you must tell your partner what kind of facilities the school has and where they are located, using position words.

Model: 我的学校有一个教学楼，两个网球场。教学楼在学校大门的左边，网球场在教学楼的后边。

你的中国学校：

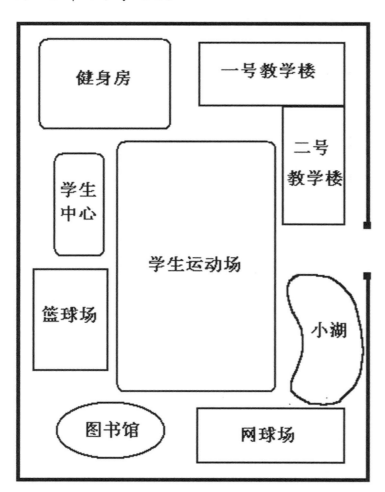

Now it's your partner's turn to describe his/her school to you. Listen carefully as s/he describes the location of each school building and then write them down on the campus map below.

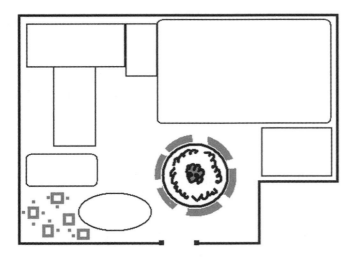

B's Sheet

Your partner will be describing his/her school to you. Listen carefully as s/he describes the location of each school building and then write them down on the campus map below.

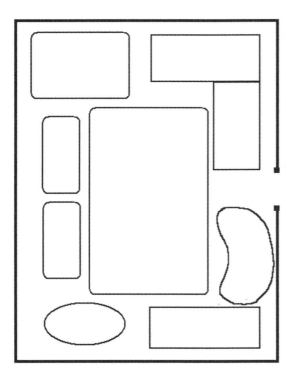

Now it's your turn to describe your school in China to your partner. In your description, you must tell your partner what kind of facilities the school has and where they are located, using position words.

Model: 我的学校有一个教学楼，两个网球场。教学楼在学校大门的左边，网球场在教学楼的后边。

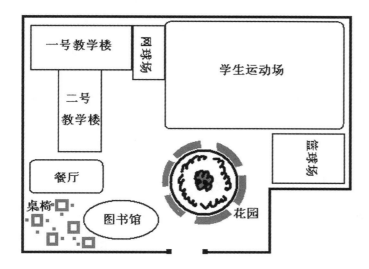

III. Pair Activity: What did you do yesterday?

Step 1: Study the activities in the table below carefully, and then circle Yes or No to indicate if you did them yesterday. Then share the results with your partner.

唱歌 Y/N	弹钢琴 Y/N	玩电脑游戏 Y/N	打篮球 Y/N	滑旱冰 Y/N
下载音乐 Y/N	做作业 Y/N	看电视 Y/N	去健身房 Y/N	看朋友 Y/N

Step 2: Now ask if your partner did the following activities yesterday. Record his/her answers in the table below.

Model: 你昨天看电影了吗？

买东西 Y/N	吃饭 Y/N	打网球 Y/N	看电视 Y/N	玩电脑游戏 Y/N
做作业 Y/N	学汉语 Y/N	去健身房 Y/N	参加排球训练 Y/N	跑步 Y/N

IV. Small Group Activity: Are you prepared for school?

Form groups of four people and complete the following interviews.

Step 1: Under each picture in the table below, indicate if you have brought the item to school today. If the answer is yes, please also write down how many. Note you MUST choose "Yes" to at least four of the items.

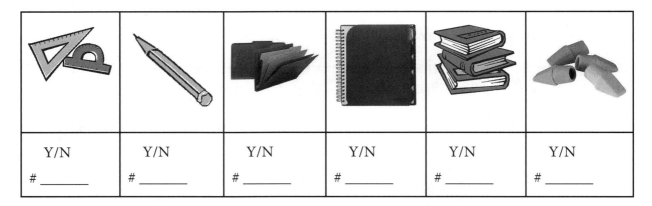

Y/N # _____	Y/N # _____	Y/N # _____	Y/N # _____	Y/N # _____	Y/N # _____

Step 2: Interview the students in your group to find out if they have brought the following school items with them today. If the answer is yes, then you will need to find out how many of each item that they have brought with them. Please listen carefully to their answers and record them in the form below.

Model: **A:** 你今天带尺子了吗？ **A:** 你今天带尺子了吗？
       B: 带了。   **B:** 没带。
       A: 你带了几把尺子？
       B: 我带了四把尺子。

学生姓名						

V. Mixer Activity: Commuter Survey

Your school is considering running school buses to pick up students in the morning. To help the school make a decision, you and your classmates volunteered to help the school conduct a commuter survey to see how many students would take the school bus if such service were provided.

Step 1: Fill out the survey below. For the purpose of this activity, assume you take public transportation to school every day. For a list of public transportation options, please refer to "学无止境" in Lesson 6.1.

Word Bank

多长时间	duōcháng shíjiān	how long a time

学生们怎么上学？

一、你家离学校远不远？

二、你每天怎么上学？

三、你上学要多长时间？

四、如果有校车，你会坐吗？

Step 2: Please interview eight classmates and briefly record their answers in the form below.

一、你家离学校远不远？
二、你每天怎么上学？
三、你上学要多长时间？
四、如果有校车，你会坐吗？

学生的名字	离学校远吗？	怎么上学？	要多长时间？	会坐校车吗？

VI. Match Them!

Match the words in Column A with the pinyin terms in Column B and their English translations in Column C.

Column A	Column B	Column C
教室	zǒu lù	train, training
前后	xùnliàn	basketball court
左右	lánqiúchǎng	restaurant, cafeteria
篮球场	qiánhòu	classroom
餐厅	zuǒyòu	front and back
走路	jiàoshì	outside
教学楼	cāntīng	tennis court
训练	jiàoxuélóu	left and right
网球场	wàibiān	classroom building
外边	wǎngqiúchǎng	walk

VII. Character Bingo

Follow the instructions for Character Bingo in Unit 4.2.

Word Bank

网球场	左边	教室	外边	教学
右边	离	教学楼	训练	后边
走路	餐厅	篮球场	前边	西边
有时候	运动	图书馆	网球队	学校

Bingo Grid

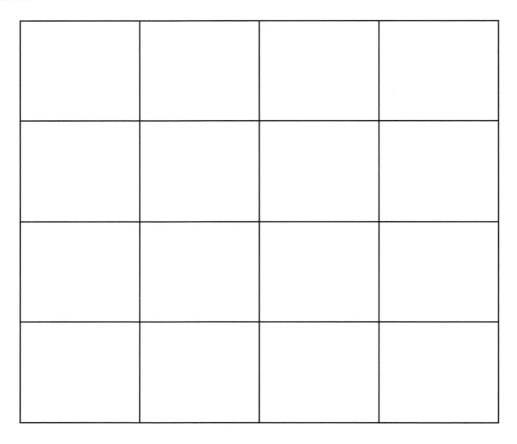

VIII. Character Crossword Puzzle

Translate the clues into Chinese characters and fill out the crossword puzzle.

Clues:

Across:

1. in the middle
2. next to school
6. in western China
7. on the left
8. west of Beijing

Down:

2. southern China
3. there is a lake in the east
5. northern China
6. on the east side
7. on the right

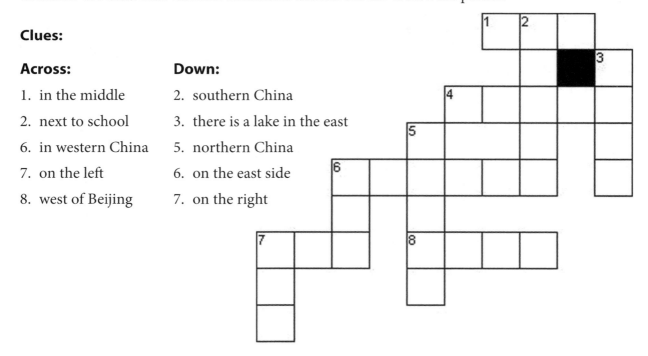

IX. **What Did Your Teacher Buy Yesterday?**

Below is a receipt from your teacher, indicating what she bought yesterday. Study the receipt carefully and then answer the questions.

王府井百货大楼购物收据		
Wangfujing Department Store Receipt		
物品名称 **Item**	数量 **Quantity**	价钱 **Subtotal ¥**
练习本	85本	85.00
汉语课本	30本	300.00
篮球	2个	120.00
尺子	25把	25.00
中国地图	6张	33.00
自行车	1辆	248.00
总计 Total		**¥ 811.00**

1. 你的汉语老师买了多少个练习本?

_____

2. 他买了多少本汉语课本?

_____

3. 他买了几个篮球?

_____

4. 他买了几把尺子?

_____

5. 他买了几张中国地图？

_____

6. 他买了几辆自行车？

_____

X.   Put the scrambled sentences into correct order, based on the English clues.

1. 篮球场 后边 在 的 图书馆

_____

(The basketball court is behind the library.)

2. 作业 她 有时候 有时候 在 在 图书馆 电脑房 做

_____

(Sometimes she does her homework in the library, and sometimes in the computer lab.)

3. 餐厅 右边 是 教学楼 的 学生

_____

(The student cafeteria is to the right of the classroom building.)

4. 离 你 远 远 学校 家 不

_____

(Is the school far from your home?)

5. 训练 你 的 吗 网球队 星期三 参加 下午

_____

(Will you come to the tennis team's training on Wednesday afternoon?)

6. 教学楼 运动场 有 餐厅 什么的 前边 电脑房
   图书馆

_____

(In front of the cafeteria, there is the classroom building, the library, the computer lab, the sports field, and so on.)

三. 汉字练习　CHINESE CHARACTER PRACTICE

姓名：＿＿＿＿＿＿＿＿＿＿

I. Write the characters in the correct stroke order.

xùn	讠							` 讠 订 训 训 (5)
训	训	训	训					
zǒu	走						一 十 土 キ キ 走 走 (7)
走	走	走	走					
lóu	木		一 十 才 木 术 术 杧 栉 柈 柈 椪 楼 楼 (13)
楼	楼	楼	楼					
tīng	厂							一 厂 厂 厅 (4)
厅	厅	厅	厅					
chǎng	土						一 十 土 圫 场 场 (6)
场	场	场	场					
yòu	口							一 ナ 才 右 右 (5)
右	右	右	右					
zuǒ	工							一 ナ ナ 左 左 (5)
左	左	左	左					
wài	夕							ノ ク 夕 列 外 (5)
外	外	外	外					

6.3 我的房间
My Room

一. 听力练习 **LISTENING PRACTICE**

I. Dictation

Listen carefully to Audio Clip 6-3-1. Each sentence will be read twice, first at normal speed for you to get a general idea, and then at slow speed for you to write down the sentence in pinyin.

1. _____

2. _____

3. _____

4. _____

5. _____

6. _____

II. **Listen to Dialogue 1 from Lesson 6.3 first and then answer the True/False questions in Audio Clip 6-3-2.**

	1	2	3	4
对				
错				

III. **Listen to Dialogue 2 from Lesson 6.3 first and then answer the True/False questions in Audio Clip 6-3-3.**

	1	2	3	4
对				
错				

IV. Listen to Audio Clip 6-2-4 and then place tone marks above each character in the poem.

月 落 乌 啼 霜 满 天，江 枫 渔 火 对 愁 眠。

姑 苏 城 外 寒 山 寺，夜 半 钟 声 到 客 船。

V. Listen carefully to Audio Clip 6-3-5. The passage will be read three times. When you listen to it for the first time, focus on the meaning of the passage and see how many characters you can recognize. The second time, underline the words that are stressed. The third time, please check your answers.

孔子说，"三人行，必有我师焉。择其善者而从之，其不善者而改之。"

Confucius said, "When three people walk together, there must be one from whom I can learn. [I can] imitate his virtuous qualities while correcting his less virtuous qualities."

VI. Listen to Audio Clip 6-3-6, in which your friend Junye, who has just arrived in San Francisco to attend an English Summer Camp, is describing his apartment to you. The audio clip will be played twice. First, focus on the main idea. Then listen to it again and mark each room in the map below.

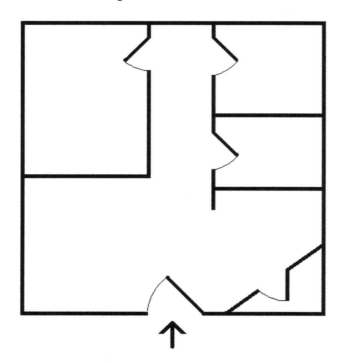

VII. Rejoinders: In this exercise you will hear parts of different conversations (Audio Clip 6-3-7). Select the expressions that best complete the conversations from the responses below.

1.

    a. 对。我们家离学校挺远的。

    b. 哪里哪里！

    c 是啊，左边是书房，右边是客厅。

2.

    a. 对。以前这是爸爸的书房。

    b. 是啊，他的房间在对面。

    c. 是啊，因为弟弟很乱。

3.

    a. 哇噻，这儿真够大的！

    b. 哎呦，卫生间在这儿呢。

    c. 真的？太好了！

4.

    a. 谢谢！

    b. 好啊！

    c. 哎呦！

5.

    a. 是啊！

    b. 哇噻！

    c. 哎呦！

VIII. Listen to the questions carefully in Audio Clip 6-3-8 and write your answers in complete sentences in the space below.

1. _____

2. _____

3. _____

4. _____

5. _____

二. 综合语言练习 INTEGRATED LANGUAGE PRACTICE

I. How do you say it in Chinese?

1. next to the dining room

_____

2. to the left of the study

_____

3. inside the bathroom

_____

4. this side of the hallway

_____

5. between the kitchen and the living room

_____

6. across from the bedroom

_____

7. Here, let me show you around.

_____

8. Wow, your house is big!

_____

9. Would you like to go take a look?

_____

10. Your room is really bright!

_____

11. You must be glad to have your own room.

_____

12. There are so many books in your study!

_____

II. **Where do you usually find these household items? Please draw lines to link pieces of furniture with the room in which they are usually placed.**

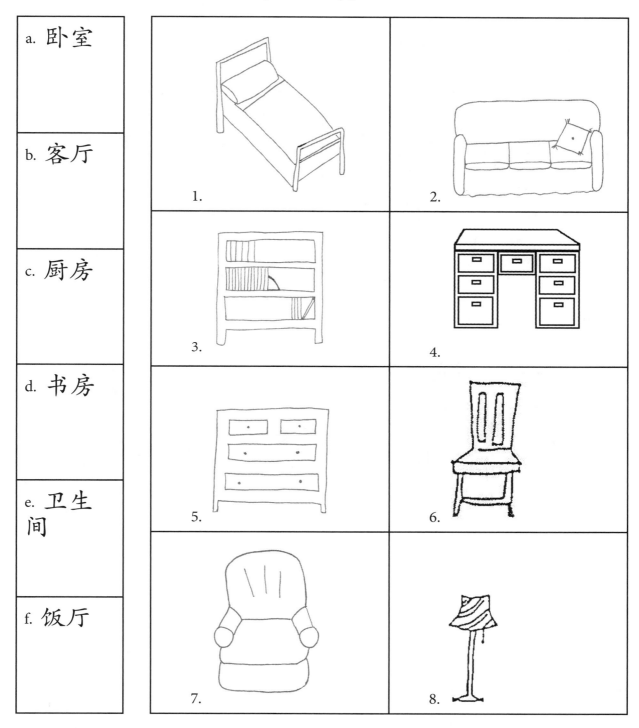

| a. 卧室 |
| b. 客厅 |
| c. 厨房 |
| d. 书房 |
| e. 卫生间 |
| f. 饭厅 |

1.
2.
3.
4.
5.
6.
7.
8.

III.   Pair Activity: I Spy

A's Sheet

Step 1: First, place the objects in the room picture by drawing lines to indicate their places. Be careful not to let your partner see your pictures.

Step 2: Play "I Spy" with your partner. According to your picture, you may say "我看见桌子下面有一只猫" or "我看见椅子上面有一本书." Your partner must place the object that you see at the proper place. You need to make sure that your partner has put the object in the correct place.

Step 3: Switch! Now it is your partner's turn to play "I Spy" with you. Listen to her/him carefully and place the objects accordingly by drawing lines using a color pencil.

Word Bank

看见   kànjiàn   to see (look and catch sight of something)

B's Sheet

Step 1: Your partner will play "I Spy" game with you. S/he will tell you "我看见桌子下面有一只猫" or "我看见椅子上面有一本书." Listen to her/him carefully and place the objects at the proper place in the room picture by drawing a line between the object and the place.

Step 2: Switch! Now it is your turn to play "I Spy" with your partner. First, place the same objects in the room picture above, using a color pencil. Be careful not let your partner see your picture.

Step 3: Play "I Spy" with your partner. According to your picture, you may say "我看见桌子下面有一只猫" or "我看见椅子上面有一本书." Your partner must place the object that you see at the proper place. You need to make sure that your partner has put the object in the correct place.

Word Bank

| 看见 | kànjiàn | to see (look and catch sight of something) |

IV. Mixer Activity: Who is your roommate?

It's the beginning of summer camp and the school has given you a housing arrangement. You know where you will be staying, but don't know who will be your roommate.

Here are two words that you may need:

| 1. 公寓 | gōngyù | apartment |
| 2. 同屋 | tóngwū | roommate |

Step 1: Pick an apartment from the four choices below. This will be your new apartment. Make sure you know how to describe it to others.

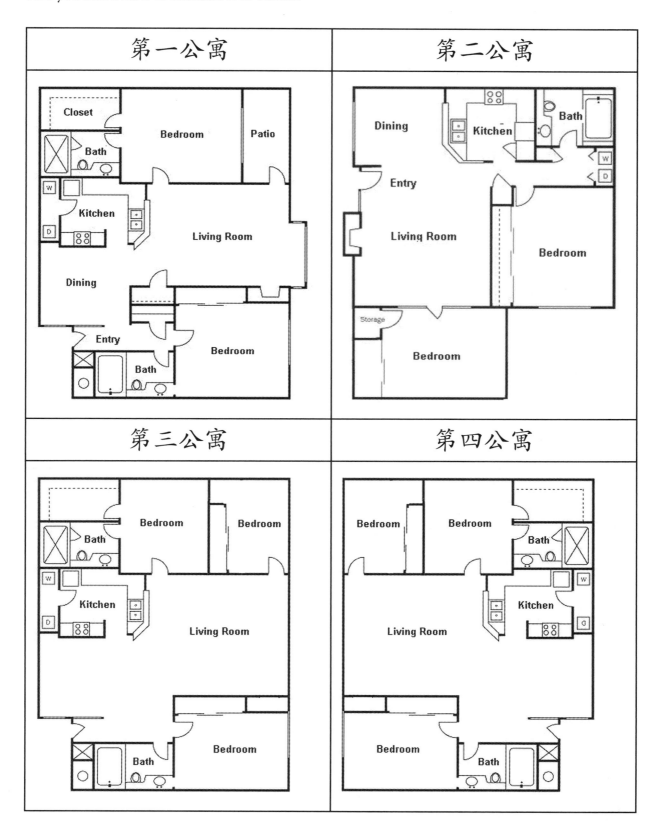

Step 2: Circulate around the classroom and describe your apartment to your classmates, until you find the person(s) whose apartment fits your description. Write your roommate(s)'s name in the space provided below:

我的同屋是： _____

V. Pair Activity: What is your house like?

Step 1: Draw a floor plan of your house, but do not let your partner see it.

★楼房: a building of two or more stories

Step 2: Ask your partner what her/his house looks like. Here are some suggested questions:

你家的房子是楼房★吗？　你家有几间卧室？

你家的客厅在什么地方？　你有自己的房间吗？

While listening to your partner's description, draw the floor plan of your partner's house.

VI. Pair Activity: Euphemisms in Chinese

Your partner has kindly shown you his/her house (in Activity V). What kind of comments would you make? You may say something in praise of his/her house. Write down at least five nice things to say to your partner.

1. _____

2. _____

3. _____

4. _____

5. _____

Now is your partner's turn to praise your house. How would you respond to the praises? Think carefully before responding.

VII. Match Them!

Match the words in Column A with the pinyin terms in Column B and their English translations in Column C.

Column A	Column B	Column C
参观	wòshì	visit (a place)
客厅	fàntīng	bright
卧室	kètīng	living room
厨房	hézhù	wow
饭厅	chúfáng	self
书房	cānguān	bedroom
卫生间	lǐ bian	inside
过道	shūfáng	messy, in disorder
房间	duìmiàn	kitchen
自己	wèishēngjiān	share a living quarter
里边	wāsai	more, even more
更	liàng	slow
对面	fángjiān	opposite, across from
整齐	dāngshí	hallway, corridor
慢	gèng	study
当时	guòdào	at that time, back then
哇噻	zhěngqí	room
合住	zìjǐ	dining room
乱	màn	bathroom
亮	luàn	tidy, in order

VIII. Character Bingo

Follow the instructions for Character Bingo in Unit 4.2.

Word Bank

房间	饭厅	亮	慢	厨房
卫生间	对面	更	整齐	乱
自己	书房	里边	过道	当时
合住	哇噻	客厅	卧室	参观

Bingo Grid

IX. **Put the scrambled sentences into correct order, based on the English clues.**

1. 你 客厅 家 真 的 漂亮

_____

(Your living room is really pretty.)

2. 一个 俩 的 中间 卫生间 我们 卧室 有

_____

(There is a bathroom between our two bedrooms.)

3. 那边 的 是 和 客厅 过道 饭厅

_____

(On the other side of the hallway is the dining room and the living room.)

4. 客厅 卧室 我 是 父母 的 的 左边

_____

(On the left of the living room is my parents' bedroom.)

5. 间 很 亮 也 这 整齐 很 书房

_____

(The study is bright and tidy.)

6. 我 姐姐 卧室 合住 当时 一间 和

_____

(Back then, my sister and I shared a bedroom.)

三. 汉字练习　CHINESE CHARACTER PRACTICE

姓名：＿＿＿＿＿＿＿＿＿＿＿＿

I. Write the characters in the correct stroke order.

| jiān | 门 | 丶 亻 门 门 问 问 间 | (7) |

间 间 间 间

| wò | 卜 | 一 丆 丆 王 王 臣 卧 卧 | (8) |

卧 卧 卧 卧

| guān | 见 | 丆 又 观 观 观 观 | (6) |

观 观 观 观

| chú | 厂 | 一 厂 厂 厂 厂 厄 厍 厨 厨 厨 厨 厨 | (12) |

厨 厨 厨 厨

| wèi | 卩 | 乛 卫 卫 | (3) |

卫 卫 卫 卫

| wa | 口 | 丨 冂 口 口 叮 叶 吐 咓 哇 | (9) |

哇 哇 哇 哇

| sāi | 口 | 丨 冂 口 口 叮 吖 咿 咗 啐 啴 喔 嗉 嘖 嗖 噻 噻 | (16) |

噻 噻 噻 噻

| zhēn | 十 | 一 十 广 市 市 声 直 直 真 真 | (10) |

真 真 真 真

| gèng | 曰 | 一 丆 币 亓 百 更 更 | (7) |

更 更 更 更

| liàng | 亠 | 丶 亠 亠 古 占 高 亭 亮 | (9) |

亮 亮 亮 亮

màn	忄						`丶 丷 忄 忄 忄 忄 忄 忄 怛 怛 慢 慢 慢 慢` (14)
慢	慢	慢	慢				

dāng	ヨ						`丨 丬 丬 当 当 当` (6)
当	当	当	当				

hé	口						`丿 人 스 合 合 合` (6)
合	合	合	合				

zì	自						`丿 亻 冃 自 自 自` (6)
自	自	自	自				

jǐ	己						`フ コ 己` (3)
己	己	己	己				

luàn	乙						`丿 二 千 舌 舌 舌 乱` (7)
乱	乱	乱	乱				

zhěng	攵						`丶 ㇖ ㇕ 口 申 吏 束 束 敕 敕 敕 整 整 整 整` (16)
整	整	整	整				

qí	二						`丶 亠 ㇒ 文 齐 齐` (6)
齐	齐	齐	齐				

II. **Word Search**

Translate the phrases or sentences into Chinese and find them in the word puzzle below.

Clues:

1. on top

_____

2. at bottom

_____

3. in front of the house

_____

4. behind the kitchen

_____

5. inside the bedroom

_____

6. outside the study

_____

7. across from the living room

_____

8. southern edge of the hallway

_____

9. north of the bathroom

_____

10. at the center of the dining room

_____

穿	穿	客	厅	对	面	房	合	议	建
过	道	南	边	洋	方	子	轻	美	剑
访	华	平	胡	讲	胜	前	重	导	面
尼	厨	房	后	面	惊	面	问	下	犯
块	获	随	率	饭	雪	资	在	件	面
苏	杨	见	期	厅	卫	座	观	外	冲
软	卧	显	晴	的	围	生	房	停	结
模	放	室	证	中	在	书	间	忍	网
实	抱	肉	里	间	上	交	云	北	队
轻	纸	奖	师	面	面	竟	总	请	边

6.4 在哪儿买汉语书？
Where to Buy a Chinese Book?

一． 听力练习 LISTENING PRACTICE

I. Dictation

Listen carefully to Audio Clip 6-4-1. Each sentence will be read twice, first at normal speed for you to get a general idea, and then at slow speed for you to write down the sentence in pinyin.

1. _____

2. _____

3. _____

4. _____

5. _____

6. _____

II. Listen to Audio Clip 6-4-2 carefully and write down each family member's name. The audio clip will be played twice.

III. Listen to Dialogue 1 from Lesson 6.4 first and then answer the True/False questions in Audio Clip 6-4-3.

	1	2	3
对			
错			

IV. Listen to Dialogue 2 from Lesson 6.4 first and then answer the True/False questions in Audio Clip 6-4-4.

	1	2	3
对			
错			

V. Listen to Audio Clip 6-4-5 and then place tone marks above each character in the poem.

朱 雀 桥 边 野 草 华，乌 衣 巷 口 夕 阳 斜。

旧 时 王 谢 堂 前 燕，飞 入 寻 常 百 姓 家。

VI. Listen carefully to Audio Clip 6-4-6. The paragraph will be read three times. When you listen to it for the first time, focus on the meaning of the passage and see how many characters you can recognize. The second time, underline the words that are stressed. The third time, please check your answers.

> 轻轻的，我走了，正如我轻轻的来；
> 我轻轻的招手，作别西天的云彩。
>
> Quietly, I leave, as quietly I arrived;
> Waving gently, I bid my "adieu" to the dusky sky.

 VII. Rejoinders: In this exercise you will hear parts of different conversations (Audio Clip 6-4-7). Select the expressions that best complete the conversations from the responses below.

1.

   a. 对不起，这是外文书店。
   b. 哎呦，我忘了。
   c. 旁边有一个银行。

2.

   a. 我想，你可以去新华书店。
   b. 我想，东风书店在银行旁边。
   c. 我想，在中山路有一个银行。

3.

   a. 那就是我常常去的书店。
   b. 那就是我常常看的电影。
   c. 那就是我常常说起的物理老师。

4.

   a. 谢谢！

   b. 是啊！

   c. 太好了！

5.

   a. 哦，左边有一个运动场，右边有电脑室。

   b. 哦，那是玛丽娅和安东尼。

   c. 哦，旁边有餐厅和宿舍。

VIII. Listen to the questions in Audio Clip 6-4-8 carefully and write your answers in complete sentences in the space below.

1. _____

2. _____

3. _____

4. _____

5. _____

6. _____

二. 综合语言练习　INTEGRATED LANGUAGE PRACTICE

I. How do you say it in Chinese?

Write down your answers or use an audio recorder to record your answers.

1. (It is) at Zhongshan Road.

_____

2. Where in Zhongshan Road?

_____

3. Which bank?

_____

4. Nice!

_____

5. Mom, look!

_____

6. Do you happen to know where I can buy textbooks?

_____

7. I think you can either go to our school bookstore or go online at Amazon.com.

_____

8. Sorry, I forgot the name of the bank. It is right next to a park.

_____

9. This is (precisely) the movie that I like.

_____

10. The kid in front of me is Maria's sister.

_____

11. Who is the one to your left?

_____

12. Which book is yours? The one on top or the one on the bottom?

_____

II. Pair Activity: Where in the World are My Cats?

A's Sheet

You have five identical cats, whose names are: 东东，西西，南南，北北 and 中中. Keeping track of where they are can be difficult. Ask your friend if s/he knows where each cat is. Listen to your friend's answers carefully and mark the location of each cat in the picture below.

Model: **A:** 你知道东东在哪儿吗？

B: 东东吗？沙发下边的是不是东东？

C: 是，是！谢谢你！

B's Sheet

Your friend has five identical cats, whose names are: 东东，西西，南南，北北 and 中中. Keeping track of where they are can be difficult. Study the picture picture carefully and answer your friend's questions regarding each cat's whereabouts.

Attention! In your answers you MUST use location words as modifiers.

Model: A: 你知道东东在哪儿吗?

B: 东东吗? 沙发下边的是不是东东?

A: 是，是! 谢谢你!

III. Pair Activity: Can you help me find my things?

A's Sheet

Help your partner to locate his/her stuff, as s/he is not the most organized person. Examine the picture below and tell your friend where the following items are:

笔　MP3　书包　书　电子游戏机

Attention! In your answers you MUST use location words as modifiers.

Model:　**A:** 你知道我的笔在哪儿吗?

　　　　　　B: 你的笔吗? 电视旁边的是不是你的笔?

　　　　　　A: 是，是! 谢谢你!

B's Sheet

You are not the most organized person and are in perpetual state of searching for your stuff. Maybe this time your friend can help. Ask your friend where each of the following items is. Listen carefully to his/her answers and mark the locations in the picture below.

Model: A: 你知道我的笔在哪儿吗？

B: 你的笔吗？电视旁边的是不是你的笔？

A: 是，是！谢谢你！

You are looking for the following items:

笔　MP3　书包　书　电子游戏机

IV. Pair Activity: Mini-Dialogues

A	B
Dialogue 1: You start. A: Ask your partner if s/he knows where you can buy some textbooks and crayons. A. Ask your friend where in Wangfujing the bookstore is located. A: Ask your friend if by any chance s/he remembers the name of the restaurant. A: Thank your friend and tell her/him that you may go to the bookstore next Sunday.	**Dialogue 1: Your partner starts.** B: Tell your partner that s/he may be able to find them in Wangfujing Bookstore. B: Tell your friend that the bookstore is located across from a restaurant. B: Tell your friend that you think it might be McDonald's.
Dialogue 2: Your partner starts. A: Tell your friend that you think New China Bookstore may have some. A: Tell your friend that it is located at West Hangzhou Road. Ask your friend if s/he knows where the street is. A: Tell your friend that the bookstore is between Bank of China and Shanghai Restaurant.	**Dialogue 2: You start.** B: Ask your friend if s/he knows where you can buy Chinese music CDs. B: Ask where New China Bookstore is located. B: Tell her/him that you know where Hangzhou Road is, but don't know where on Hangzhou Road the bookstore is. B: Thank your friend and tell her/him that you may stop by the bookstore this weekend.

V. Your Chinese friend wants to learn what American students usually do on weekends. She has asked you to share a snapshot of you and friends. Please bring a photo from your album. On a separate sheet of paper, write a letter to your friend, using location words to tell her who is in your picture and, if there is a background scenery in the photo, briefly describe the scenery.

Expressions you may use:

你看，这是我和朋友们的照片。

我左边的人是玛丽娅。

玛丽娅后边的学生是安东尼。

我们的后边是学校的篮球场。篮球场左边的楼是教学楼。

VI. Small Group Activity: Spot the Trend

As part of your internship you are helping a marketing firm conduct a survey among your peers on the most popular products/places/activities among teenagers.

Step 1: Form a group of four. Sit facing each other.

Step 2: Ask the person sitting across from you the following questions. Record her/his answers in the space provided.

问题：

1. 你常常去的书店是哪个？

_____

2. 你常常看的书是哪些？

_____

3. 你常常玩的电脑游戏是哪些？

_____

4. 你常常看的电视节目是什么？

_____

5. 你常常听的音乐是什么？

_____

6. 你常常吃的快餐是什么？

_____

7. 你常常去买东西的商店是哪些？

_____

Step 3: Now interview the person sitting on your left. Record her/his answers in the space given.

问题：

1. 你常常去的书店是哪个？

_____

2. 你常常看的书是哪些？

_____

3. 你常常玩的电脑游戏是哪些？

_____

4. 你常常看的电视节目是什么？

_____

5. 你常常听的音乐是什么？

_____

6. 你常常吃的快餐是什么？

_____

7. 你常常去买东西的商店是哪些？

_____

Step 4: Finally, turn to the person in your group whom you haven't talked to and interview him/her.

问题：

1. 你常常去的书店是哪个？

_____

2. 你常常看的书是哪些？

_____

3. 你常常玩的电脑游戏是哪些？

_____

4. 你常常看的电视节目是什么？

_____

5. 你常常听的音乐是什么？

_____

6. 你常常吃的快餐是什么？

_____

7. 你常常去买东西的商店是哪些?

_____

Step 5: Examine the results from your interviews. Can you spot the trend? What do those interviewees have in common? Please fill out the following report:

我问了_____个同学。他们_____

_____

_____

_____

_____

_____

_____

_____

_____

_____

VII. Match Them!

Match the words in Column A with the pinyin terms in Column B and their English translations in Column C.

Column A	Column B	Column C
银行	duìwài	or
照片	jiàokēshū	textbook (formal)
对外	wàiwén	photo
忘	shūdiàn	foreign language
或者	huòzhě	(oriented towards) overseas, abroad
外文	yínháng	bank
书店	wàng	forget
教科书	zhàopiàn	bookstore

VIII. Character Bingo

Follow the instructions for Character Bingo in Unit 4.2.

Word Bank

教科书	书店	对外	银行	照片
外文	左边	右边	常常	漂亮
或者	周末	旁边	饭店	名字
知道	对面	饭店	不错	许多

Bingo Grid

IX. **Put the scrambled sentences into correct order, based on the English clues.**

1. 知道 在 吗 你 什么 书店 地方 外文

_____

(Do you know where the Foreign Language Bookstore is?)

2. 东风 左边 的 中国 一个 书店 饭店 有

_____

(On the left side of the East Wind Bookstore, there is a Chinese restaurant.)

3. 学校 是 的 这 我们 照片

_____

(This is a picture of our school.)

4. 有 银行 许多 里边 人

_____

(There are many people in the bank.)

5. 法语 你 去 可以 外文 买 书店 教科书

_____

(You can go to the Foreign Language Bookstore to buy French textbooks.)

三. 汉字练习　CHINESE CHARACTER PRACTICE

姓名：_____

I. Write the characters in the correct stroke order.

kē　禾	ノ 二 千 禾 禾 禾 科 科 科 (9)	
科 科 科 科		
diàn　广	、 一 广 广 庄 庄 店 店 (8)	
店 店 店 店		
huò　戈	一 厂 厂 戸 写 或 或 或 (8)	
或 或 或 或		
zhě　耂	一 十 土 耂 耂 者 者 者 (8)	
者 者 者 者		
yín　钅	ノ ト ヒ 乍 钅 钊 钊 钊 铟 银 银 (11)	
银 银 银 银		
fàn　饣	ノ ク 饣 饣 饣 饭 饭 (7)	
饭 饭 饭 饭		
wàng　心	、 亠 亡 产 忘 忘 忘 (7)	
忘 忘 忘 忘		
zhào　灬	丨 冂 日 日 旷 昭 昭 昭 照 照 照 照 照 (13)	
照 照 照 照		

II. **Character Crossword Puzzle**

Clues:

Across:

3. The one next to the kitchen is mine.

4. The notebook under the backpack belongs to Nina.

5. Where is your room?

6. The chair in front of the computer is not very good.

Down:

1. His book is the one on top of the desk.

2. Dongdong is the cat behind the TV.

6.5 请来参加我的晚会
Please Come to My Party

一. 听力练习 LISTENING PRACTICE

I. Dictation: Listen carefully to Audio Clip 6-5-1. Each sentence will be read twice, first at normal speed for you to get a general idea, and then at slow speed for you to write down the sentence in pinyin.

1. _____

2. _____

3. _____

4. _____

5. _____

II. Dictation: Listen to Audio Clip 6-5-2 carefully. The paragraph will be read twice, first in normal speed for you to get a general idea, second in slow speed for you to write down in pinyin.

_____

_____

_____

_____

_____

III. Listen to Audio Clip 6-5-3 and then place tone marks above each character in the poem.

清 明 时 节 雨 纷 纷，路 上 行 人 欲 断 魂，

借 问 酒 家 何 处 有，牧 童 遥 指 杏 花 村。

IV. Listen to the recording of Dialogue 1 from Lesson 6.5 first, and then answer the True/ False questions in Audio Clip 6-5-4.

	1	2	3	4	5
对					
错					

V. Listen to the recording of Dialogue 2 from Lesson 6.5 first, and then answer the True/ False questions in Audio Clip 6-5-5.

	1	2	3	4	5
对					
错					

VI. Linda, Mark, and Mary are talking about their summer vacation plans. Listen to Audio Clip 6-5-6 and find out what each person would like to do. Please write down their plans in the table below.

	林达	马克	玛丽
参加数学班			
去加拿大玩儿			
去北京看朋友			
学习中国武术			
玩电脑游戏			
回英国看父母			
游泳			
看很多书			
去南京旅游			
听音乐会			

 VII. Rejoinders: In this exercise you will hear parts of different conversations (Audio Clip 6-5-7). Select the expressions that best complete the conversations from the responses below.

1.

a. 星期六晚上七点半。

b. 在学校餐厅。

c. 我家对面是咖啡馆。

2.

a. 国际学校的老师和学生。

b. 我们要带什么？

c. 暑假我去北京。

3.

a. 我们去溜冰，好吗？

b. 他要去北京看姥姥。

c. 我要去香港看父母。

4.

a. 他欢迎我们去他家玩。

b. 不，你们应该多学习。

c. 我可以每天休息。

5.

a. 是的。

b. 我不要可口可乐，我要冰水。

c. 他要喝什么？

二. 综合语言练习　INTEGRATED LANGUAGE PRACTICE

I. Read the following lyrics after listening to Audio Clip 6-5-8. This is a folk song from the Sala ethnic minority in Qinghai province. Afterwards, use the same poetic or musical format and some colorful words to describe a thing or a place. Share it with your classmates.

			Ā	Lǐ	Mǎ	Yā			
			阿	里	玛	呀			
Bō	xià	de	zhǒng	zi	shì	bái	bái	de,
播	下	的	种	子	是	白	白	的，
chū	lái	de	yá	ér	shì	lǜ	lǜ	de,
出	来	的	芽	儿	是	绿	绿	的，
kāi	kāi	de	huā	ér	shì	hóng	hóng	de,
开	开	的	花	儿	是	红	红	的，
jiē	xià	de	guǒ	ér	shì	huáng	huáng	de.
结	下	的	果	儿	是	黄	黄	的。

New Words

阿里玛	ālǐmǎ	name of a berry
播	bō	plant
种子	zhǒngzi	seed
芽	yá	bud, sprout
结	jiē	bear (fruit)
果	guǒ	fruit

▌▌. How do you say it in Chinese?

Write down your answers or use an audio recorder to record your answers.

1. Are you coming to my party this Saturday afternoon?

_____

2. The party is at David's house. His address is 6550 First Street.

_____

3. Welcome to my house. Please come in.

_____

4. What do you plan to do during the summer vacation?

_____

5. I am going to visit my grandparents in Shanghai.

_____

6. My mother wants me to take a music class during the summer vacation.

_____

7. After working for twelve hours, his father needs to take a rest.

_____

8. In July, I am returning to the US to visit friends.

_____

9. I don't allow my cat to drink Coca-cola.

_____

10. You should drink less coffee.

_____

III. Pair Activity: Where exactly is the French Café?

A's Sheet

You and your friends are going to meet at the French Café. Everyone says it is difficult to find this small café because it is located in a crowded city block. You've emailed a friend who has been there before to find out exactly where it is, but his reply is quite vague. You decide to call him and get more information.

Step 1: Use the information in your friend's email to ask questions.

Model: **A:** 书店是不是在咖啡馆的对面？(try to use 是不是)
            B: 不是。书店在咖啡馆的左边。

Reply	Reply All	Forward	Print	Save	Junk	Delete

那个法国咖啡馆旁边有书店、小公园、银行、饭店、文具店什么的。咖啡馆很小，可是外边也可以坐。我觉得坐在外边更好玩，你们坐在外边吧。

Step 2: Listen to your friend's answer carefully and try to draw a sketch of the café's location.

人民路			
	🏛 法国咖啡馆		

B's Sheet

Your friend is calling you to find out about the exact location of the French Café. You went there once but didn't pay too much attention to its surroundings. Fortunately, you found a business card from the café that has a sketch on the back. Use the sketch to tell your friend where the café is.

日本饭店	中国饭店	小公园	
人民路			
新华书店	🏛 法国咖啡馆	民生银行	新新文具商店

IV. Pair Activity: Planning a Party

You and your partner are in the organizing committee for an end of the school year party. In order to give a great party, you decide first to come up with some ideas individually and then to put your ideas together.

Step 1: Using the table below to write down a few ideas about the party. Write your ideas in Column 1.

Step 2: Based on what you wrote, take turns to tell your partner about your ideal party.

Step 3: Listen to your partner's ideas and write them in Column 2.

Step 4: Based on your ideas, reach a decision on what the party should be like.

	你	你朋友	你们俩的决定 (your final decision)
请谁来参加?			
在哪儿?			
什么时候?			
吃的东西			
喝的东西			
活动			
其他 (other)			

V. Write an Invitation

Based on your decisions in Activity IV, write a party invitation to your principal on a separate sheet of paper. You may use the space below to take notes on what you want to write. Your note should include the following:

1. When and where the party will be held;

2. Who will be at the party;

_____

3. What kinds of refreshments will be served;

_____

4. What activities are planned for the party; and

_____

5. Special requests to the principal (if any).

_____

VI. Mixer Activity: Summer Plan

Suppose you are helping a newspaper to conduct a poll on students' summer life and their understanding of responsibilities. Your job is to interview at least four students, record their responses, and report one activity that most students would like to do and one activity that they think they should do.

Step 1: Write down in the space below three activities that you plan to do in the summer.

暑假的时候，我想：

1. _____

2. _____

3. _____

Step 2: Go around the classroom to interview at least four students. Ask them 暑假你想做什么, record their answers, and ask a follow-up question 你应该…吗?

Model: 你：暑假你想做什么？
你朋友：我想休息。
你：你觉得自己应该休息吗？
你朋友：应该。

Step 3: Go over your results and circle the item that has gotten the most responses.

Step 4: Report to class one item from each column (想，应该) that most students you talked to have agreed on.

学生暑假生活调查		
暑假你想做什么？	应该	不应该

Word Bank

调查　diàochá　survey

VII. Pair Activity: Mini-Dialogues

A	B
Dialogue 1: You start A: Ask your partner if s/he would like to come to your house for a party. A. Tell your friend your home address and try to describe what is around your house. A: Tell your friend that if s/he can bring some music CDs, it will be great.	**Dialogue 1** B: You are delighted to go the party. Ask when and where the party will be. B: Ask your friend if you should bring some soft drinks or food. B: Tell your friend you will bring some CDs and thank him/her for inviting you.
Dialogue 2 A: Tell your friend that David is going to visit his friends. A: Tell your friend that David is planning to travel to Xi'an and Chongqing. Ask your friend if s/he plans to travel as well. A: Ask your friend where s/he will work. A: Tell your friend that you would like to work, but your parents want you to study history and math this summer.	**Dialogue 2: You start** B: Ask your friend if s/he knows that David is going to Beijing during the summer vacation. B: Ask if David is going to do some travel. B: Tell your friend you will work in the summer. B: Tell your friend that you will work in a bookstore. Ask your friend if s/he will work too.

VIII. Match Them!

Match the words in Column A with the pinyin terms in Column B and their English translations in Column C.

Column A	Column B	Column C
喝	kāi	have (a meeting, party, conference)
商店	kāfēiguǎn	cup, glass (a measure word)
真	zhēn	cafe, coffee house
问题	shāngdiàn	question
进	jiù	drink
暑假	Jiānádà	enter, come in
杯	bēi	Canada
姥姥	jìn	shop, store
咖啡馆	shǔjià	really
加拿大	Kěkǒukělè	plan
开	lǎolao	Coca-cola
打算	hē	summer vacation
可口可乐	wèntí	exactly, precisely
就	dǎsuàn	maternal grandmother

IX. Character Bingo

Follow the instructions for Character Bingo in Unit 4.2.

Word Bank

开	暑假	商店	请坐	姥姥
打算	可口可乐	喝	等	问题
进来	咖啡馆	真	杯	欢迎
休息	武术	游泳	冰水	加拿大

Bingo Grid

X. Put the scrambled sentences into correct order, based on the English clues.

1. 暑假 去 他 看 姥姥 香港

_____

(During the summer vacation, he will visit his grandmother in Hong Kong.)

2. 晚上 在 我 晚会 明天 家 七点 开

_____

(There is a party at my house at 7 p.m. tomorrow.)

3. 他 冰水 要 我 喝 要 可口可乐 喝

_____

(I want some ice water and he wants some Coca-cola.)

4. 妈妈 我 学 和 物理 要 数学

_____

(My mother wants me to study math and physics.)

5. 晚会 欢迎 我 你 生日 参加 的 来

_____

(Welcome to my birthday party.)

三. 汉字练习 CHINESE CHARACTER PRACTICE

姓名：＿＿＿＿＿＿＿＿＿＿

I. **Write the characters in the correct stroke order.**

kāi 廾	一 二 于 开 (4)
开 开 开 开	

shāng 口	丶 亠 产 产 产 商 商 商 (11)
商 商 商 商	

kā 口	丨 口 口 叮 叻 咖 咖 咖 (8)
咖 咖 咖 咖	

fēi 口	丨 口 口 叮 咁 咁 唪 唪 啡 啡 啡 (11)
啡 啡 啡 啡	

guǎn 饣	丿 夕 夕 夕 夕 饣 馆 馆 馆 馆 馆 (11)
馆 馆 馆 馆	

tí 页	丨 口 日 日 旦 早 早 昺 是 是 趷 趷 题 题 题 (15)
题 题 题 题	

jìn 辶	一 二 于 井 井 讲 进 (7)
进 进 进 进	

hē 口	丨 口 口 叮 叩 吗 呾 呾 唱 喝 喝 喝 (12)
喝 喝 喝 喝	

shǔ 日	丨 口 日 日 旦 早 里 昦 昦 暑 暑 暑 (12)
暑 暑 暑 暑	

jià 亻	丿 亻 亻 亻 作 作 作 作 作 假 假 (11)
假 假 假 假	

suàn	竹					ノ ← ← ← ⺮ ⺮ ⺮ 笄 笃 笡 筲 **筲** 算 算 (14)
算	算	算	算			

lǎo	女					ㄑ ⼥ 女 女 ⼥ 女 妙 姥 姥 (9)
姥	姥	姥	姥			

6.6 第六单元复习
Review of Unit 6

综合语言练习　INTEGRATED LANGUAGE PRACTICE

I. After reading Text 1 from Lesson 6.6, answer the questions in Audio Clip 6-6-1. Write down the questions in pinyin while you are listening, and then answer them in Chinese.

1. 问题：_____

   回答：_____

2. 问题：_____

   回答：_____

3. 问题：_____

   回答：_____

4. 问题：_____

   回答：_____

5. 问题：_____

   回答：_____

Word Bank

回答	huídá	answer

II. Your Chinese pen pal has asked you to describe your home and your neighborhood. In your letter, please write about your surroundings in general, and then discuss one particular aspect that you like or dislike. Use specific examples to justify your opinion. To help with your letter writing, you can use the template below.

亲爱的笔友：你好！

祝你

学习快乐！

你的笔友，＿＿＿＿＿＿＿＿＿

年　月　日

III. Pair Activity: Where do they live?

Lin Fang (林芳), Xiao Ming (小明), Xie Xiaolan (谢小兰) and Xiao Ma (小马) are neighbors. Following the clues, match the person with the house where he/she lives. You should work in pairs to solve this puzzle. Please try to use only Chinese in the process.

	第一个房子	第二个房子	第三个房子	第四个房子
姓名				
职业				
宠物				

他们住在哪儿？

Clues:

小马是美术老师。

音乐老师养了一只猫。

养狗的人不是女的。

林芳住在美术老师家左边的房子里。

谢小兰的金鱼不喜欢旁边房子里的古典音乐。

小马不喜欢鸟。

中文老师的八哥鸟很怕住在右边房子里的狗。

小明住在3号。

Word Bank

1. 八哥鸟 bāgēniǎo parrot	2. 美术 měishù fine arts	3. 职业 zhíyè profession

IV. **Mixer Activity: Your Quality of Life**

You are conducting a survey on the quality of life among secondary school students. Please circulate around your classroom and interview your classmates on the topic.

Step 1: Before starting your interview, please answer the following questions for yourself.

1. 你每天几点上学，几点下学？

2. 你每天晚上做什么？

3. 你周末做什么？

4. 你昨天运动了吗？

5. 你家的前后左右有什么？

6. 你每天怎么上学？

7. 你的学校离你家远不远？

8. 你每天上学要多长时间？

Step 2: Interview at least three students. Listen to their answers carefully and record them in the space given below.

第一个学生：

1. 你每天几点上学，几点下学？

2. 你周末做什么？

3. 你昨天运动了吗？

4. 你家的前后左右有什么？

5. 你的学校离你家远不远？

第二个学生：

1. 你每天晚上做什么？

2. 你昨天运动了吗？

3. 你家的前后左右有什么？

4. 你每天怎么上学？

5. 你每天上学要多上时间？

第三个学生：

1. 你每天几点上学，几点下学？

2. 你每天晚上做什么？

3. 你昨天运动了吗？

4. 你家的前后左右有什么？

5. 你的学校离你家远不远？

三. 汉字练习　CHINESE CHARACTER PRACTICE

姓名：＿＿＿＿＿＿＿＿＿＿＿＿＿

I. Write the characters in the correct stroke order.

mài	十			一 十 士 吉 吉 吉 卖 卖 (8)
卖	卖	卖	卖	
zhǔ	、			、 二 亍 主 主 (5)
主	主	主	主	